Historical Sketch of the
Chemung Valley New York

Elmira and Chemung County

and Broome, Herkimer, Livingston, Montgomery, Onondaga, Ontario, Otsego, Schoharie, Schuyler, Steuben, Tioga, Ulster Counties

by T. Apoleon Cheney

First published in 1868

Reprinted with an index
by New York History Review, 2017

Historical sketch of the Chemung Valley, New York: Elmira and Chemung County, New York and Broome, Herkimer, Livingston, Montgomery, Onondaga, Ontario, Otsego, Schoharie, Schuyler, Steuben, Tioga, Ulster Counties

by T. Apoleon Cheney, originally published in 1868, and new index added by New York History Review, 2017

Copyright © 2017 Reprinted by New York History Review. Notice of Rights. **Some rights reserved.** No part of this book may be reproduced or transmitted in any form by any means, electronic, mechanical, photocopying, recording. or otherwise, with the prior permission of the author.

For information on getting permission for reprints and excerpts, contact us through our website: www.NewYorkHistoryReview.com

First Edition
ISBN: 978-0-9965353-9-7

Table of Contents

Chapter I..7

Chapter II..19

Chapter III...31

Chapter IV...37

Chapter V..55

Chapter VI...149

Note...179

Index..181

To William Cullen Bryant

CHAPTER I

Introductory remarks: - Occupation of our country by the Aboriginal tribes - Early Discoveries and Expeditions made by the French and English in the region of Western New York, etc.

The Chemung Valley, and the adjacent region has already been assigned a prominent place in the domain of history, of romance, and of song. It would indeed appear vain and futile to attempt to make collection of any unrecorded facts, or to narrate any of the thrilling stories that the pioneer still relates of the olden time that can add to the interest that already attaches to the famed and almost classic ground. But, the strangely beautiful legends, the romantic myths, connected with the period of the Revolution, which various historical, as well as other literary works, had recorded of this beautiful and picturesque valley, has served to awaken and stimulate further researches about its history.

The writer of this sketch had first, indulged the hope to be able to collect material that would form reliable basis for a somewhat full and complete history of the region that had been the theatre where one of the strangest and most interesting dramas of past time had been enacted, but the haze which in long intervening years had gathered around its marvelous scenes, renders any complete narrative of its important and changing events, or of the actors who participated in them, now impossible. It may also be mentioned that whilst the writer was pursuing, in the early part of the summer of 1865, extended inquiries and investigations respecting the early history of the section which includes the beautiful inland lakes of our state, illness had interposed to prevent further research or attention to the subject; and now, after the lapse of many months, the choice only seems to remain to him, either to give a rough and desultory sketch of the events which he has already acquired information, some disconnected outline of incidents in the history of this region, or to permit them to slumber in oblivion. It will be my only object to give a simple and truthful relation of facts. For all imperfections of style, which otherwise might challenge criticism, I must ask for generous allowance and indulgence. This sketch is, only a humble contribution to the history of the valley lying between the Chemung River and the Seneca Lake, also, giving a partial record of the thrilling legends of the adjoining country that is inseparably blended with the early history of the valley.

The men of the Revolution have passed away. The pioneers of our country are no more. The noble endurance which these men who had entered and subdued the wilderness displayed, teaching the virgin soil to bud and bloom with the beauty of a new Eden, is worthy of eulogium only surpassed by that paid to the patriots and heroes who had achieved our national independence. They all repose beneath the green and fragrant turf - alike slumbering in their honored graves.

Over this region, within the historic period, four great empires have claimed the sovereignty - four great powers that have exacted submission to their imperial sway. Scarcely a century has passed by since the earliest of these dominant powers, the proud Iroquois confederacy, held the mastery over the broad forestlands which divided the waters of the continent; here the Conhocton, the Canisteo, and other streams, rushing along the fertile valleys until joining the noble Susquehanna, they, at last, mingle with the ocean; there, the waters which formed the beautiful lakes, seeking an outlet through the magnificent Ontario, and majestic St. Lawrence, until they too reached the great Atlantic; while upon its western borders, the rivers, fed by springs among the hills of Steuben, united their currents to give tribute to the monarch of floods, whose waters giving verdure to all the broad lands of the imperial West, welcomed in embrace at last the queenly seas of the tropics.

I needs must pause to glance one moment at this remarkable power, this great Empire of the past. This unrivalled Indian confederation, which had been acquiring strength, and power, and greatness, for three hundred years before the culmination of its grandeur at the period of the Revolution, was preceded by an empire of yet older date, which in unknown time held the continent in its imperial grasp, the monuments reared by this lost empire, in some far and unknown time, which still perpetuate some indistinct record of its former greatness, can only be traced in the mounds, and military earthworks that have been found existing throughout our country, including the region occupied by the Iroquois. To this subject; however, I cannot do better than introduce extracts from, letters which I had the honor to receive from several eminent scholars, the most illustrious scientific men of our land, whose valuable opinion will possess much greater interest than views which only a student in this department of investigation like myself, could advance. The late Benjamin Silliman, LL.D., Emeritus Professor in honored Yale, and who during the last half century had occupied the most distinguished, the most illustrious position among the scientific men not only of America, but of the world; thus, referring to the mounds, writes:

> *I believe they were not erected by the ancestors of our Aborigines, but by a people greatly advanced in civilization and arts, like the*

Mexicans. I saw on Salisbury's plain in England, numerous mounds belonging no doubt to the same state of society with those in the west of America. I counted more than seventy in one view - the largest called King Silberry's Mound, was 180 feet high, and its base covered nearly an acre of ground. It is described in my travels in England in 1805. You are aware that in the middle and north of Europe there are on the continent many sepulchral mounds. They appear to be characteristic of a particular era in social advancement. Another distinguished scholar who also had ranked among the first historians in our country, Jared Sparks, LL.D., in a letter dated February 26, 1862, gives expression of his views: "These monuments are not more curious as specimens of antiquity, than as furnishing a clue to the history of the race of men by whom they were formed. It is a striking fact that scarcely any mounds or other antiquities of the kind, have been found between the Allegheny Mountains and the Atlantic Ocean, while they are so numerous in the region of the West. It would seem to imply different races who had little intercourse with each other." Moreover, concerning the history and antiquities of the reaction occupied by the Iroquois, H. R. Schoolcraft, LL.D., whose long continued Archeological and Ethnological investigations were embodied in various able and elaborate publications, beside the great national work, issued in six quarto volumes, "History, Condition, and Prospects of the Indian Tribes of the United States," in a communication to the writer of this article says: "There is nothing in our history more interesting than our Indian antiquities, and we are just beginning to get some reliable light upon the subject. We have made extravagant speculations upon the subject; but, it requires to be studied from another and closer point of view. The ancient tribes of Indians were more populous, and had a higher degree of arts than our modern tribes. Europe only began really to make acquaintance with them in 1608. The French had proceeded no farther than Lake Champlain when they encountered the Iroquois in 1609. The same year the Dutch landed in Albany, and they were followed by the English after a lapse of fifty years."

Again, the distinguished historian of the Indian race, in a letter of August 3, 1863, but a short time before his decease, writes;

"Your memoir on Indian antiquities of western New York was received; it entitles you to the thanks of all who make researches into our Aboriginal history. The Vesperic tribes who settled in the present area of the United States, were in their physique, and in their mental organization, manners and arts, I think, of one race, and the antiquities they have left to us are of corresponding unity, and those persons who imagine that the antiquities of the Mississippi Valley differ essentially from those of Eastern America must furnish stronger proof than those hitherto adduced. The Iroquois came from the south up the Ohio Valley, and after following down the St. Lawrence to near the mouth, with their capital at Hochelega, planted themselves in western New York, in the center of the Algonquin nations. Here, they were at the sources of the great rivers of the country, and soon made their presence felt. However, I have not leisure to pursue this interesting theme.

It will be noticed that the views entertained by the distinguished scientists that I have named, about the race or races of men that had once occupied our country, do not fully correspond: they are no less valuable as furnishing aid to our enquiries. The learned and distinguished ethnologist, Dr. S. G. Morton who bad made extensive and profound investigation of this subject - in the elaborate examination of the physiological traits and precise measurement of crania obtained from every section of the continent, every Indian nation-arrived at the opinion, expressed in his great work, *"Crania Americana"* that the various nations, or tribes, inhabiting the continent were composed of but one race of men. A scientific examination of craniological characteristics of osteological remains that may be exhumed hereafter from the unexplored mounds in our country, may however yet furnish evidence to overthrow the physical indicia referred to for the unity of races that has held sway upon the Western Hemisphere.

Intrusive elements of European civilization and art have occasionally been discovered within the country occupied by the Iroquois who unquestionably date before the expeditions of the early French Missions. Among these traces of early European occupation, was the singular relic found in the Onondaga country, a boulder upon which was inscribed - "Leo VI. 1520" - which it will be seen dates some eight years before De Soto's discovery of the Floridas. The Scandinavian sages relate that about A. D. 1000, the Northmen coasted along the Eastern shores of America, until they reached a country that they designated - *Vineland*; this is included in the *Transactions of the Royal Society of Northern Antiquaries*. The writer of this sketch had opportunity to examine, both during the progress of the survey of ancient monuments of western New York, and since its termination, several relics which could only be referred to very early European occupation or expeditions; the late Honorable Edward Everett who had ably reviewed the *Antiquates Americanae*, in a letter written soon alter they had come to my notice, remarked, that he "had never supposed that the Northmen were thought to have penetrated to Western New York," and that the relic in question "indicates a more recent date." The literature of Europe, both including and subsequent to its classic era, in the myths, and the poetical, as well as historical narratives it contains, is richly suggestive of some vague knowledge of a continent lying in the bosom of the western ocean, well known to the ancient Phoenicians, Carthaginians, and Tryrians, and visited in 1147, 1170, in 1380, by various navigators - the lost Atlantis, of which history first acquired reliable knowledge at the time of its discovery by Columbus who in reaching the *Ultima Thiule* realized the prediction in the *Media* of Seneca. However, the great Tower that once ruled the country, and had reared the fast decaying monuments still disclosed throughout our wide land, has passed away. Such an event certainly affords one of the strangest, one of the grandest problems in human history; and gives scope for the most profound philosophical research. Histories are often only records of battles and campaigns, of the movements of kings - Cæsar's that

*"Get the start of this majestic world,
And bear the palm alone..."*

but, here we have the "reverse, there is not an annal, not a single written record, which traces the story, for future times, of this great empire of the past. Only the vast and crumbling monuments of the west point to its remote antiquity - only the figures, the deities, chiseled in the stone that have been left us, with their cold moveless lips, are eloquent with the myths, the traditions of its glory.

The Iroquois, originally composed of five nations, and afterward by the ascension of 1612 of the Tuscaroras of the Six Nations, presented an anomalous feature in the history of the Indian race; their confederation bears comparison, in some respects, to the Amphictyonic league described in the classics; while they have been styled the *"Romans of the West."* The name Aquinoshioni [Iroquois], or Long-house, by which the confederacy was designated, also represents its policy or national character. The Iroquois also styled themselves, the Ongni-Honni; as the Empire State, the successors to the departed power have adopted the motto of similar import - "Excelsior." The traditions of these people indicate their origin and success to Taronyawagan - the Divinity who protected this nation - and who was known as Hiawatha. Around their central council fire, at Onondaga, were shown the noblest qualities of the "Hunter Race"; here was exhibited a sagacious national policy, military ardor, and eloquence in debate, which has been indeed unrivaled in Indian history The writer of this sketch has had somewhat ample opportunity to become acquainted with the Indian character, derived from personal observation; the Iroquois possessed the manlier virtues of the hunter state of society - a magnimity of thought and action, love of liberty, heroism in danger, and a stoicism in suffering-and sometimes a simplicity, a poetic grandeur, and sublimity in expression of thought and sentiment, which could only be born amid his native forests. Nevertheless, from the mental observations which the Indian exhibits, as has been observed in an able work, written by a distinguished statesman of our country, the Honorable Lewis Cass, about "the moral character and feelings of the Indians, of their mental discipline, and of all that is most valuable to man, in history of men, we are about as ignorant as when Jacques Cartier first ascended the St. Lawrence."

The Iroquois had attracted the early attention of men in command of European expeditions to this country. In 1534, Cartier, under the authority of the King of France, had penetrated the region occupied by the Iroquois; and on his return to France published a glowing account of the expedition. In 1535, he conducted another expedition to the Iroquois country. Toward the close of the seventeenth century, Father Hennepin had made a tour through the country held by the Iroquois, and in his narrative published soon after termination of the Expedition, in France, and again in first Volume of *Transcriptions of American Antiquarian Society,* in 1820, he thus speaks of the power of the Iroquois: "They would never cease from disturbing the repose of the Europeans, were it not for fear of their firearms. For they entertain no commerce with them unless it is firearms, which they buy on purpose to war against their neighbors; and by which they have extended their bloody conquests five or six hundred leagues beyond their own precincts, exterminating whatever nation they hate."

A work written in Latin and published at Paris in 1664, states that a French colony was established in the country of the Iroquois about the year 1655. Charlevoix, in his *History of New France,* also mentions that missionaries were sent to Onondaga in 1654. The Iroquois held the balance of power in America. In 1608, Champlain had laid the foundation for Quebec. A hundred and fifty-two years passed away while the conflict was being waged by the French and English monarchs for the supremacy of the American continent. This contest is fully traced in the volumes of the *Colonial History of New York.* In 1759, Niagara yielded to the assault of the British army; and upon the heights of Abraham, opposite Quebec, Wolfe and Montcalm each were struggling to gain the victory which should decide the long battle for the domination of the continent, and with his dying hand, the English general snatched the Bourbon-lilies from the flag that henceforth should wave over the Canadas. The proud French capital of the New World, Quebec, had capitulated upon September 18, 1759; and with its surrender, the gorgeous dream of founding a colossal Empire, New France, upon the western continent, vanished forever.

It should have been mentioned in referring to the French claim of the territory of the Iroquois, as belonging to New France, which this remarkable confederation of warriors had successfully resisted the objects sought to be attained by the expedition of De La Bare, and of De Nonville. At subsequent time, Count Frontenac, an able governor of Canada, conducted his expedition against the Iroquois. On June 16, 1696, this expedition left Quebec, and on August 4, the army arrived at the principal town of the Onondagas, and formed in array of battle, but the Indians who could have brought six or seven hundred warriors to defense of their Fort, nevertheless burned this entrenchment, with their wigwams, &c., and precipitately fled. The Indian cornfields, and other means of subsistence, were destroyed by orders of Count Frontenac. A detachment under command of M. de Vandreville, to destroy the Oneida town, having successfully accomplished their mission, returned on August 9 to the main army. This expedition reached Montreal on August 20 in its return from the Iroquois campaign, and on September 12 arrived at Quebec. This expedition under command of Count Frontenac, has furnished, in the romantic incidents connected with it, a theme which had inspired the muse of one of the most gifted poets of our country, Alfred B. Street - his genius has wrought out this subject in the beautiful and elaborate poem *Frontenac*. However, I shall have the occasion again to refer more fully to this expedition. In the especial relation, it sustains in the history of the Senecas, and in connection with the widely named Queen of this nation.

At the period of the Revolution, and to the poem illustrating this interesting episode of Indian story, in the subsequent pages of this sketch.

It was only a year before the fall of the French capital, Quebec, that Captain Ponchet who had commanded the engineers at the successful assault upon Oswego, New York, in 1756, and was afterward engaged in the construction of Fort Niagara, while stationed at that very renowned fortification in 1758 compiled the map - *Carte des Frontiers, et Angloises deus le Canada depuis Montréal jusques on Fort du Quense*; it is a rough map. Drawn from information, as stated in his dispatch accompanying the map of April 14, 1758, obtained at Niagara (*Colonial Documents*, page 624, Vol. X.) This map delineates the region of country particularly embraced in these investigations; it represents the river St Lawrence and Lake Ontario - the Seneca Lake is here laid down by name of Kanantage, the Cayuga Lake as Kendais. An Indian town or castle, Ocyendahit is marked on map lying between the two lakes above referred to an Indian trail is traced upon the map as passing from Fort Niagara by Kaensataque (Canandaigua) through the Indian village between the lakes, then up the valley of Catharine Creek until reaching the source of this stream, and thence rising upon the hills and leading to Knacto (Painted Post, New York) at the junction of the river here laid down as Kaygen (Tioga) and the River de Kanesto (Canisteo, New York), thence through Knacto Castle to Fort du Quense. An Indian village, Thaggen, is marked upon the map at the confluence of *de Kanacto* and the *Branche est de la Susquehanna*. This is undoubtedly the earliest chart that delineates the lakes and streams, the mountains, and plains, of this picturesque region, then covered by the boundless forests of which the lied man was the only monarch. In the year following the date of this map, the overthrow of the French at Quebec terminated the great struggle for the dominion of the continent, which would be deemed worthy, if a Homer still lived, of the epic numbers of an Iliad.

CHAPTER II

Early French Expedition to the headwaters of the Chemung, and Border Warfare in this Region - The Early Settlement and History of the Canisteo and Conhocton Valleys

It was a balmy morning in early June, as I stood upon the picturesque shore of the river, where the waters of the Conhocton, blend with those of the Canisteo to form the noble Chemung; but a few miles farther up this pleasant valley, where the forests have given place to cultivated fields, the Tioga (the stream designated by Sir W. Johnson as the Cayuga Branch) unites with the Canisteo River. This is rich historic ground. It was, but a brief time after the French had relinquished their claim to New France, that an expedition was sent by the English into this region, and from this date, we have no longer to deal with dim and uncertain myths of Indian prowess, and imperfect legends of French expeditions, in tracing the history of this section of country, earlier; its records, no longer obscured with darkness that had rested upon the continent, now assume their proper place amid the annals of the historic time. It appears, from the VII volume of *Colonial Documents* that two subjects of the British king, while passing, in the year 1762, through the country of the Senecas, were murdered by two Indians living at the village of Kanisteo which was settled by Shawnees and Delawares, "stragglers from several tribes." Sir W. Johnson, upon learning of this occurrence, sent Lieutenant Guy Johnson with a party to Onondaga Castle, where they arrived on December 4, to demand the surrender of the murderers. On the 7th, the council gave an answer, the "chief speaker of Onondaga," Teyewarunte, delivering the reply that as the Village of Kanisteo was under jurisdiction of the Six Nations, if the Senecas did not deliver the murderers, then the other tribes would do so. This promise, however, was only made to be broken; another council was held the following year at Johnson's Hall, at which this matter was brought up by Sir W. Johnson, and earnestly pressed upon the attention of the Indian Sachems present - forty-two of their principal chiefs - but without resulting in the delivery of the murderers. Accordingly, the Iroquois who were sincerely attached to the English, at request of Sir W. Johnson, determined upon signal retribution to the vagrant Indians residing along the Kanisteo. And, on April 1, 1764, Captain Montour, a son of the Indian queen, Catharine Montour, and who had earlier signalized his name, as we ascertain in consulting Vols. VI, VII, and VIII, of *Colonial Documents*, in conferences with the Indians at Onondaga, and at Fort Johnson, and as being in command of various parties of the Iroquois, as at the German Flatts in 1758 - with a hundred warriors set out from Oquago (the town of Windsor in Broome County, New York) on the Susquehanna River, for destroying the villages of the Delawares &c., located upon the tributaries of this river, the Kanisteo and other streams. They successfully accomplished within two weeks the object of the expedition. Sir W. Johnson, in a communication dated April 28, 1764, to Lieutenant Governor Colden, gives the following succinct narrative of this hostile excursion:

> *The first instant, Captain Montour with 140 Indians and a few white men, set out from Oquago, and on arriving at the first of the enemy's towns found the same abandoned, which he burned. It consisted of thirty-six houses, built of square logs, with good chimneys; thence he went to and burned another of thirty houses with four villages, and then proceeded to Kanisteo, which he likewise*

destroyed. It consisted of sixty good houses, with three or four fireplaces in each of them. Here and at the other towns, he found a large quantity of Indian corn, which he destroyed, &c. (Vol. VII, *Colonial Documents*).

There are reasons to suppose, from the situation of the Indian towns marked on Pouchet's map, and descriptions of the Indians' towns elsewhere given, that the first village which Captain Montour reduced to ashes is identical with the one designated on the map is Knacto (Painted Post) and he then proceeded to destroy an intermediate Indian town, and then the castle, or village of Canisteo. Captain Montour, the leader of this early raid into the Canisteo Valley, was afterward present at the conference held at Fort Stanwix in 1768, when Sir W. Johnson negotiated a treaty with the Six Nations, securing an extensive cession of lands as marked on the map drawn at the time, in large red lines. This map was corrected from Raveuis' earlier map. It is a striking historical coincidence, that this point at the confluence of the Conhocton and Canisteo, rendered famous in our annals at such an early date, as the scene of the brilliant exploit of this chieftain of the forest, Montour, who might rival the bold excursions of some chivalrous knight of the middle ages, should, after the lapse of many years, be the place where this chief was buried, and become so widely famed as the spot where his comrades reared the rude monument recording his achievements - the "Painted Post." During the summer of 1779, a large party of Tories and Indians, commanded by the loyalist, McDonald, and the Seneca chief, Hiakatoo, made a fearful incursion among the border settlements of the Susquehanna, when they had successfully attacked Freeling's Fort, but in a skirmish with the hardy yeoman under command of Captain H. Boone, the Tories and Indians suffered a great loss, and returned from this raid with many wounded, via the Tioga, and beneath the broad elms where the Canisteo and Conhocton met, Captain Montour, the gallant warrior and chief of the Senecas who had been wounded in the conflict with the brave borderers, expired; and his brethren of the wilderness made his grave by the river's side, and above the last resting place of the warrior they reared a post, upon which they inscribed or painted various rude devices and symbols, and this rude monument was afterwards often visited by the braves of the Senecas, and other tribes. This post disappeared about 1810, as we are informed in the *History of Steuben County*. The place where it had stood is still well known. A few miles from this place, in the northeastern part of the town of Corning, New York is the "Old Indian Tree," beneath whose shade the Red Men have passed many hours in worship of the Great Spirit.

    It was upon the banks of the Canisteo - whose waters now murmur and glide swiftly by me, then rip along the fairy land which lies below - that amid the Revolutionary War, in 1779, the pine trees were hewn down and fitted into large canoes, and when they were all launched upon this stream, then were embarked upon this earliest-fleet that had traversed its eddies, the- savage warriors and renowned chiefs of the Six Nations, the Butlers with their still more savage renegades and barbarians, and gaily dressed and accoutered with weapons of war, all ride in this mysterious armada down the river, along its dark gorges and beneath the shadows of over-hanging elms, then swiftly descend upon the strong, rapid currents of the Chemung, until the long file of boats disappeared amid the hills that border the noble Susquehanna. It was this strange fleet that gliding amid the light of day and amid the darkness of night, upon the waters of the Canisteo, whose brawling eddies dare not reveal the fearful mission of this squadron that carried the party which in 1778, lay waste the lovely valley of Wyoming [Pennsylvania] - the rude armament that had borne destruction to the peaceful hamlets of this enchanting region.

William Harris was the first pioneer of Steuben County. He came up the Chemung River soon after the close of the Revolutionary War, and erected at Painted Post the first building occupied by civilized man within the present boundaries of Steuben, the most western habitation of the white man then in the southern tier of New York. The Indians assisted him in building this cabin. Harris was a merchant, and sold his wares to the Red Men of the forest, early in the spring of 1787. Judge Barker, the pioneer of Urbana, found Harris at Painted Post, and on the Christmas following, upon going again to that place, he found the cabin of Harris burned, and Harris, the Robinson Crusoe of the wilderness, too, was gone; but the trader was only temporarily absent, and afterward returned to Painted Post, where he lived many years. Here, when Judge Baker was making an excursion into the wilderness beyond the Tioga, there was a solitary cabin near the junction of Cowanesque with Tioga River. Frederick Calkins, from Vermont, was the first farmer that settled in Steuben County. He located near the Chimney Narrows, in 1788. Eli Mead was the first supervisor of the town of Painted Post, then comprised in Ontario County, and he went to Canandaigua to attend the annual meeting of the Board of Supervisors. Mr. Fuller kept the old Painted Post Tavern; a house built of round logs, with two apartments, one story in height.

Among the noted pioneers of Steuben County, toward the close of the last [18th] century should be mentioned Benjamin Patterson, the renowned hunter. He was born in Virginia in 1759, and was a relative of Daniel Boone. In early life, he had removed to the region of the Susquehanna where his taste for hunting was acquired. During the Revolutionary War, he was attached to a company of riflemen that was engaged in defense of the frontier settlements. He was at the skirmish of Freeling's Fort, before referred to. He was attached to the party commanded by Captain Hawkins Boone, and there had a perilous escape. He, likewise, was connected with the party of rangers that pursued the Indians along the Chemung and its tributary streams. He participated in the border warfare of the Revolution, its adventures and bold conflicts; and at the termination of the war he chose his home among the wild woods of the Conhocton. The unexplored and trackless wilderness, the rifle his only companion, was indeed a home to his free adventurous spirit. He often led emigrants through the wild labyrinths of the forest, to the promised lands beyond the famed country of the Genesee. Formerly, he guided Talleyrand, the accomplished and distinguished diplomatist, through the forests of this region. About 1796, he took his goods in a boat up to the Painted Post, and for many years, or until about 1805, kept the old hotel at Knoxville. It is said that he ran the first raft upon the waters of the Canisteo. In the year 1800, C. Hulburt built an ark, and loading it with wheat, with his primitive boat descended the Canisteo, and the larger rivers below, to Baltimore, Maryland. Benjamin Patterson died at Painted Post, in 1830, closing an eventful career of which numerous romantic incidents, strange and thrilling reminiscences, are yet related by the inhabitants of this region. The first store at Painted Post, at which goods were sold to the settlers, was kept by B. Eaton. He brought his first assortment of merchandise from Wattle's Ferry (now Unadilla, New York) in two canoes. Among the early pioneers of the old town of Painted Post which was purchased of Phelps & Gorham in 1790 were Judge Knox, from New Jersey in 1793, and Captain L. Erwin and Colonel A. Erwin from Ireland, and who served in the American army in the Revolution, in 1794; also. J. Winter, a hunter.

Painted Post was erected into a town in 1796; in 1804 taxable inhabitants was 130, the assessment roll, $2,004.53. Its total tax $293. In 1852, the old historical name of Painted Post was changed to Corning. I could not gather full information respecting the various newspapers that had been printed at Painted Post. The *Painted Post Herald* was commenced in March 1848, D. C. Lumbard, editor - the *Corning Journal* was established January 1, 1845, the *Corning Democrat* was established in 1846. The population of Corning now exceeds six thousand inhabitants.

In 1788, a small party, consisting of S. Bennett, Uriah Stephens, K. Crosby and Captain J. Jamison, commenced a tour of exploration up the Chemung Valley, and of the Conhocton, but found no situation which answered their anticipations, until striking across the densely wooded hills lying south of the Conhocton, they came to "the valley of the Canisteo." Standing on the precipitous brow of a hill overlooking this valley, through which the river glided amid the majestic elms, graceful maples, and dark pines that were growing upon its banks in wild and magnificent grandeur - a prospect of unrivaled and fascinating beauty was at once presented; while farther down this valley there was an open extent of several hundred acres, covered only with tall, wild grass, and luxuriant flowers - as if some God had removed from the west one of its beautiful prairies, and placed it here. In the Indian's traditional lore, there existed no reminiscences regarding the origin of this meadow; the Red Men said that it had existed here from time immemorial. In this strangely beautiful vale- amid this magnificent scenery, which even now in its picturesque outline of romantic hill and swiftly flowing river, at once arrests the artist's eye - and as I stand here this balmy summer day, thrills every nerve with pleasure:

> "There is a pleasure in the pathless woods,
> A rapture on the lonely shore."

was indeed a favorable spot to commence a new settlement; and here this party of hardy pioneers selected their future home. In the autumn of 1789, Crosby and Stephens, with portions of their respective families, after a toilsome voyage up the rifts of the river, arrived at the place of their proposed settlement on the upper Canisteo. They immediately went into the forest, cut down the trees, and built a house of logs, 24 x 20 feet in dimension, containing a singe apartment illuminated by the blaze of crackling limbers in four large fire places, one being in each corner of the room.

Here, the two families passed the winter of 1789-90, and in the ensuing spring were joined by S. Bennet, Colonel J. Stephens, &c. Mr. S. Bennet built in 1793 the first grist upon the Canisteo or rather, it was erected on Bennet's Creek, about a half mile from its junction with the Canisteo. The first tavern on the Canisteo was established about the year 1810, by George Hornell (Judge Hornell) and J. Stephens, a Baptist preacher, below Bennet's creek. Solomon Bennet was the first captain of the earliest military organization in Steuben County. Upon the river banks of the Canisteo, and among the surrounding hills, were nurtured a race of yeomen, of bold adventurers, an athletic, boisterous, rough, and daring class of men who could run, wrestle, or fight that would not have done dishonor to the brave barons of the Old World; and the rude, stout settlers who participated and gloried in the adventures of chivalrous daring, always ready to take share in the Olympic amusements of the borders, had soon established the fame of "Canisteer" throughout this region of country. Maybe some future Walter Scott may gather up these legends of the forest, of the bold borderers that have now passed away, and weave them into song. On November 21, 1788, Massachusetts had conveyed to Oliver Phelps and Nathaniel Gorham, for consideration of three hundred thousand pounds, all its right, title and interest in lands that now constitute the counties of

Steuben, Yates, Ontario, part of Wayne, part of Monroe, also portions of Genesee, Livingston and Allegany, containing some 2,000,000 acres. The Indian title to this immense estate had been purchased by Phelps and Gorham, in deed dated November 18, 1790, conveyed to Robert Morris, of Philadelphia, all their lands then remaining unsold, amounting to over a million of acres. Robert Morris, by deed hearing date April 11, 1792, conveyed to Charles Williamson a million and two hundred thousand acres. Williamson was agent of Sir William Pultney, England. Sir W. Pultney was a son of James Johnstone, and assumed the name of Pultney on his marriage with Mrs. Pultney, niece of the Earl of Bath. Sitting in their princely mansions in London, the British baronet and his associates, built a gorgeous dream. Before them flitted a vision of the city that should rise, with its castles and busy marts upon the upper tributaries of the Susquehanna. This city that they would rear in the wilderness, outrivaling the brilliant achievements of a Caliban, should, by a commercial stratagem, take the key of success from Quebec and New York, and become the proud metropolis of the continent. Never before had such a gorgeous, brilliant air-castle floated before human eyes! Captain Charles Williamson, a gentleman of talent, of energy, and spirit, versatile and impetuous, was selected to fulfill this enterprise, to turn into reality the golden dream whose hues were mirrored upon the Western sky. He arrived at Baltimore in 1791, and ere long established his central quarters, preparatory to building this metropolis of the wildwoods, at Northumberland, on the Susquehanna, at the junction of the West Branch. In the beautiful valley of the Conhocton some sixteen miles from the confluence of the river with the Canisteo, to form the noble Chemung in a picturesque situation where the valley assumed a wide extent, near the waters of a fairy little lake, which glistened in the sunlight like some fabulous stream of the Orient - Captain Williamson determined to locate his future city, to erect its walls and build its bastions.

In 1793, he commenced building the village here - which he named Bath [New York], in honor of Lady Bath. Before the close of the season, fifteen families had become residents of the new settlement. The first tavern was constructed of pine logs, in two apartments, one story in height. It was kept by a family named Metcalf. Mr. Sherman Metcalf afterwards removed to Ellicottville, New York. William Dunn, upon the southeast corner of the Public Square, opened another house of entertainment. Mr. Cruger, from Denmark, next occupied this tavern. Charles Cameron from Scotland kept the first store in the village. He was also the first postmaster; the mail being brought once a week from Northumberland (as stated by General McClure in his narrative of the early settlement of Bath). Robert Campbell, D. McKinsie, H. McElwn, Charles McClure, &c., were among the early pioneers of this section. About 1794, Captain Williamson established a theatre at Bath. In 1796, he caused a racecourse, one mile in circuit, to be constructed near the village. On the day appointed for the first race, some two thousand persons had assembled- sportsmen from Virginia, New Jersey, Maryland, from Philadelphia, and New York, were there to enter the lists. These races added much to the renown of the "Village of the Plains." In 1795, the Conhocton River was explored and partially cleared of obstructions. George McClure built an ark 75 feet in length by sixteen in breadth, and loading it with a cargo of staves run it down the river. This was the first raft that had navigated its waters.

However, this baronial stronghold, in its infancy, was threatened with destruction. Captain Williamson had become interested in the settlement at Sodus. He received from Colonel Simcoe, Governor of Canada, a warlike note demanding that he should immediately relinquish his designs, &c. The administration at Washington assumed charge of the matter, and required Captain Williamson to place his village in position of defense. Several blockhouses, and an entrenched position surrounded by picket defense, were put in course of immediate construction. Several pieces of artillery and a thousand stand of arms were ordered from Albany [New York]. A regiment composed of some five or six hundred men, was organized, Williamson receiving commission as colonel. The forces were drilled and instructed in the art of war, and a guard was stationed every night to prevent surprise. Bath, indeed, presented a military attitude. However, the hostile British expeditions did not make descent from the frowning fortresses of Niagara and Oswego, of which the English still kept possession. Bath was not besieged; the threatened war did not ensue.

Steuben was organized into a separate county, the six towns comprising it being taken from Ontario County in 1796. The first Court of Common Pleas was convened on June 21, 1796, William Kersey presiding judge. The court was held in the new court house, a framed building. Among the lawyers present were N. W. Howell, Vincent Mathews, William Verplanck, Thomas Morris, &c. Among the early members of the Steuben County Bar were George D. Cooper, William Stuart, David Jones, D. T. Blake, S. T. Haight, and in subsequent years, Daniel Cruger, W. B. Rochester, Henry Welles, H. W. Rogers and Edward Howell, ranked among the prominent members of the legal fraternity. In 1802, Colonel Williamson's agency of the Pultney estate, terminated, Robert Troupe, Esq., succeeded to this agency. In 1807 the Reverend John Niles, a Congregational minister who in 1803 had settled at Prattsburg, New York, was employed to preach every alternate Sabbath at Bath, New York. Among the prominent men who came to the county at an early date, were Samuel Baker (afterward Judge) Captain John Sheather, (an officer in the Revolution and a favorite of General Washington) Captain Joel Pratt, Judge Porter, Silas Wheeler (who was one of the men under command of Arnold in his march through the wilderness in the expedition to Quebec, and was near Montgomery, when in the assault upon the British fortifications the

American general fell mortally wounded) and Colonel Lindley, the pioneer of Tioga Valley.

In 1796, the *Bath Gazette and Genesee Advertiser* was published by William Kersey, and James Eddie. This was the first newspaper printed in western New York. The same year another paper, *Ontario Gazette*, was established at Geneva. The *Bath Gazette* had a list of some five hundred subscribers, but was only published for a brief time. In 1810, Benjamin Smead commenced the publication at Bath, of the *Steuben and Allegany Patriot*, which I believe was continued some twenty-five years. In 1815, David Rumsey commenced the publication of the *Steuben Farmer's Advocate*. The *Steuben Courier* was commenced at Bath, in 1843, and it is still published at this place. The *Temperance Gem*, edited by Jennie and Caroline Rumsey, was started in 1854. In 1804, the taxable inhabitants of Bath were 119; its assessment roll $2,739.23. The population now numbers some 5,300. The first buildings in Bath were constructed of logs. These were succeeded by modest framed houses. Since 1840, when I had passed through this village, I notice that many elegant edifices, tasteful suburban residences, have added to the attractions of this rural village. And, as I stand upon the hills south of this pleasant village, the rays of the declining summer sun resting upon the sweet lake below, and the circular range of abrupt and lofty hills, covered with green fields, and luxuriant woodland, only broken by that gorge upon the north, with its hazy vista opening to the fairy valley of the "Crooked Lake" [Keuka Lake] that stretches dimly away in graceful but indistinct outlines; I feel, I realize all the beauty of this scene; but, upon the glowing canvass, and not upon this paper, can its loveliness be pictured.

CHAPTER III

Early History of the region adjoining Chemung Valley lying on Susquehanna River - The Massacre at Wyoming in 1778 - Indian raids at Cherry Valley, and other places upon the Headwaters of the Susquehanna which led to the organization of Sullivan's Expedition.

A beautiful day had passed while I leisurely descended the Conhocton and the Chemung - passed like the waters of this majestic river that are gliding by.

"*The wave I gaze on now returns no more.*"

Another balmy day has come, and as I stand musing by the side of the river, a few miles below Elmira [New York], imagination too, glides away with these rapidly rushing waters, through the pleasant vales and dim vitas that lie in the distance, until it becomes blended with the early historical reminiscences of the valley of Wyoming. This is indeed to our memory classical ground. In childhood, I had read with delight Campbell's beautiful poem, *Gertrude of Wyoming*, and its picturesque description of the pastoral happiness and quiet that had made its home here, lingered in my recollections:

"*Delightful Wyoming! Beneath thy skies*

*The happy Shepherd swains had naught to do
But feed their flocks on green declivities."*

In the *Columbiad*, I find its author, Barlow, thus refers to the expedition of the Tories and Indians that laid this valley at waste:

*"His savage hordes, the murderous Johnson leads.
Files through the woods, and treads the tangled weeds."*

I can only wander over this interesting, historic ground for a moment. It was reserved for the pen of our country's most gifted and eminent poet, whose genius has wed the literature of our land to immortal fame, to picture this valley in all its loveliness, and recall its thrilling historical reminiscences, which has been so beautifully and truthfully done in Halleck's *Wyoming*. Thus reads the closing stanza:

*"And on the margin of yon orchard hill
Are marks where timeworn battlements have been.
And, in the tall grass traces linger still
Of arrowy 'frieze and wedged ravelin.'
Five hundred of her brave that valley green
Trod on the morn in soldier-spirit gay
But, twenty lived to tell the noonday scene -
And, where are now the twenty? Passed away.
Has death no triumph hours, save on the battle day?"*

In the last line of this fascinating poem, quoted above, America's illustrious poet has expressed, or rather suggested thoughts, not less poetical, than of profound philosophical, and historical significance. However,

I cannot dwell upon the scenes connected with this valley except as they may relate to events that have transpired in the region particularly embraced in our historical enquiries. As early as 1742, the devout missionary, Zinzendorf, commenced his worthy labors among the Indians of this region, winning the unlettered children of the forest to the pure faith of the Christian religion. In 1753, an association for making a settlement in the Wyoming Valley [Pennsylvania] was organized in Connecticut, which held claim to this section under its ancient charter. This association also purchased the title of lands bordering on the Susquehanna, at an Indian council held at Albany in 1754. The Pennsylvanians, however, claimed jurisdiction of this territory under the grant made to William Penn. Resulting from this conflict of authority, arose in succeeding years, contests, and border wars, with varying triumphs, and defeats that would have been worthy of the middle ages- worthy of that era when valiant Knight, with his mailed retainers, bravely battled to defend the fair fame of Lady-love.

The annals of this region have been traced respectively by Chapman, Heckwelder, Miner, Stone and Peck. I will recall an episode in the strange history of the Wyoming Valley, or Westmoreland, as it had become known. The record of the siege of the several forts, the battle, the surrender, and the tragic massacre that occurred here in the first days of July 1778, has become familiar as household words in American history. Upon the night succeeding the battle, terrific scenes were enacted. Amid the darkness and gloom of midnight, Queen Esther, with the fiends who did her bidding, performed the fearful orgies of guilt and blood, not unlike the weird crimes, the dark incantations of Hecate in the witch's cave. The bloody rock where this priestess of blood sacrificed the lives of innocent human beings, however, had assumed in the present fearful drama, the place of the "boiling cauldron," around which witches performed the mysterious, damning "deed without a name." Queen Esther, as mentioned on page 176 of Miner's *History of Wyoming,* resided upon the banks of the Susquehanna in "sullen retirement," her palace being located near the confluence of the Tioga with the Susquehanna, within the precincts of Westmoreland. A large number - about a hundred fugitives, women, and children, escaped from the settlement, and in the darkness of night, without provisions, and many of 'them without clothing, fled through the wilderness for safety - while they stifled the hunger which they buffered in the hope of preserving their lives. This flight presents a scene of dramatic interest rarely surpassed in history.

 I have thus glanced at the thrilling events that occurred in this Valley in 1778, because they had been the principal agency, together with British and Indian atrocities committed in the preceding year in Tryon County, the expeditions led by St. Léger and Brant in the Mohawk Valley, in awakening the retribution visited them in 1779. In November 1778, Butler and Brant, with their followers made a descent upon Cherry Valley [New York]. Thirty-two inhabitants, women, and children were killed, besides several men composing the garrison, being massacred. Mrs. Campbell, with her children, was carried into captivity. The family was separated at the time they were made prisoners, but were reunited at Niagara, with the exception of one child, James S. Campbell, then six years of age; but he, after an interval of two years of captivity among the Indians in Canada, was restored to his mother at Montreal. He afterwards became widely known as the Honorable J. S. Campbell, and his elegant residence at Cherry Valley was built upon the site of the old family mansion that in the Revolutionary War, had been used as a fort. His son, the Honorable William W. Campbell, late Justice of the Court of Appeals, and author of *Annals of Tryon County,* &c., thus writes me, April 18, 1865, about his venerable parent: "My father, James S. Campbell, is still living. He lives with me at this place - Cherry Valley; is now in his 93rd year, and is still hale and well." The prowess of the Iroquois confederacy had received some check at Fort Stanwix, and at the Battle of Oriskany, where the intrepid General Herkimer was wounded. However, hostile expeditions continued to be made throughout the summer and autumn of 1778, among the border settlements, as at the German Flatts, and in the Schoharie Country.

These events which I have briefly noticed, led to the organization of the expedition under command of General Sullivan in 1779, which destroyed the Indian towns in Western New York, and effectually crushed the Indian power within their once proud and hitherto unconquered domain.

CHAPTER IV

The Organization of Campaign of 1779 against the Indians of Western New York, by General Washington; the principal command of Expedition assigned to General John Sullivan - The American Army ascend the Valley of Chemung, defeat the allied British and Indians - Precise locality of the Battle-ground- Farther progress of the army in the country of the Iroquois - Destruction of the Indian town at Genesee, and return of the Expedition, &c.

The sagacious and comprehensive mind of Washington had originated, as the effectual defense against Indian hostility, the master policy of the decisive campaign of 1779, carrying the warfare against the Indians in accordance with the only mode in which it can be successfully waged. This mode, however, was not strictly in accordance with military rules laid down by European Tacticians; on the contrary, it adopted the Indian manner of fighting - following the enemy into their strongholds, burning their towns, and destroying their means of subsistence. The command of the expedition against the Six Nations was entrusted to General John Sullivan. It had first, been proposed that General Gates should have direction of this command, but the intention subsequently was abandoned. General Sullivan was born in Berwick, Maine in 1740. Arriving at mature years, he read law, and removed to New Hampshire. He was a delegate to the first Continental Congress, and was afterwards engaged in command of the expedition that captured Fort William and Mary, at Portsmouth. He was one among the eight brigadier generals who Congress appointed in 1775, and in 1770 received appointment as Major

General in the Continental Army. In 1777 he was engaged in the battles of Brandywine and Germantown, and in the winter of 1777-78, assumed command of the troops of Rhode Island, and conducted the expedition against Newport in August of 1778.

The Assembly of the State of Rhode Island in February 1779 - as will be seen in Vol. VIII of *Records of the State of Rhode Island* had voted their thanks to General Sullivan, in consideration "of the active zeal with which he hath exerted the forces under him, for the preservation of this State, and the security of its inhabitants" - (page 508, VII Vol. of *Records*), briefly, had been the history of General Sullivan, before his receiving the appointment to take chief command of the army designed for the overthrow of the vast and powerful Indian confederacy which hitherto had been the successful ally of the English in the terrible warfare waged upon the border settlements, as the desolated hamlets of the German Flatts, Fort Plain, Stone Arabia, Cherry Valley, Unadilla, Minisink, and other places within Tryon and Ulster counties, whose names have indeed become classic in the annals of the Revolution, so fearfully attested.

General Sullivan, in a communication dated April 16, 1779, in a very able manner submitted his views relative to the proposed expedition, to General Washington, the Commander-in Chief of the American Army, and the opinions advanced in this letter were substantially adopted in the arrangement of this important campaign. This paper will be seen on page 264. Vol. II, of *Correspondence of the American Revolution*, edited by Jared Sparks; and it affords, as the results of the campaign have shown, ample proof of the superior military skill and knowledge of the officer who had been assigned command of this expedition against the Six Nations.

General Washington whose masterly skill and judgment in the prosecution of warfare against the Indians, had been evinced upon the battleground near the Monongahela [River], where on the memorial July 9, 1765, the army of Braddock were led into ambuscade by the subtle warriors of the forest, and were only, after the fall of General Braddock, rescued from entire destruction by the bravery and skill of Washington- had proposed to carry the terrors and calamities of war into the Iroquois' own domain, destroy their strongholds and burn their towns, in a communication to Congress, January 12, 1779, most ably urged the importance of this movement as the only efficient protection to the patriots in all the border towns of New York and Pennsylvania. Washington was only in his seventeenth year when he began his explorations in the Indian territory beyond the Alleghenies, which he continued for several years, being engaged in diplomatic as well as military excursions among the Western tribes, and had thus acquired a thorough knowledge of the Indian character, and which afterward became of such indispensable avail to the cause of the Revolution shown by his wisdom in originating and planning the campaigns against the Indians, and which conduced in an eminent degree to our national success in the struggle for Independence.

It was arranged that the principal division of the Army designed for the invasion of the Indian country should proceed under immediate command of General Sullivan, along the Susquehanna toward the headwaters of this majestic river, where upon its confluence with the Tioga it would be joined by another division under command of General James Clinton - and thence, in combined array, march into the populous Indian country. It may be remarked, that General James Clinton was born in Ulster County in 1736. At the age of twenty, then holding rank as Captain, was engaged in the assault upon Fort Frontenac; received appointment of Colonel in 1775, and participated in the expedition to Canada under General Montgomery. In 1776, he was appointed Brigadier General, and was actively engaged in service connected with the war until 1779, when he became associated with General Sullivan in the expedition against the western Indians. The name, the family of the Clintons has indeed become one of the most illustrious known in American history. George Clinton, a brother of General James Clinton here referred to, occupied the important position as governor of New York during the war of the Revolution; and in a communication to General Washington, dated May 18, 1779, had given his views, in an able and comprehensive manner, relative to military arrangements required for successful prosecution of the intended campaign against the Six Nations. De Witt Clinton, a son of General James Clinton, it need scarcely be said, acquired enduring and preeminent fame as one of the ablest among the many distinguished statesmen who at various times have held the place as governor of New York, without mentioning other learned and eminent men more recently connected with this family. General Clinton, with five brigades having numerical strength of 1600, commenced his march on June 17 from Canajoharie, New York, his *point d'appui* in the Mohawk Valley, across a hilly country to Otsego Lake; but this lake, owing to the drought of summer season, would not admit of the passage of his boats, amounting to 220 *batteaux*, and carrying a park of artillery, stores and provisions over its waters, and General Clinton had resource to constructing a dam across the lower portion of the Lake, thus raising its waters to such extent that upon removal of the artificial obstruction, the accumulated floods rapidly carried his armament to its destination; and on August 22 he formed a junction with the main division under General Sullivan which had ascended the Susquehanna, at Tioga point, and their united force now amounted to five thousand men - the respective brigades under command of Clinton, Hand, Maxwell, Poor and Proctor. Some time earlier, General Schuyler had communicated intelligence to Clinton, that the enemy were already aware of the objects of this expedition; the allied British and Indian forces, had made ample preparations for defense, and erected entrenchments on the Chemung, where they awaited the approach of the American army. From the year 1634, when Cartier had ascended the St. Lawrence, and erected upon its shores the standard of the French King, the French and English had contended for the possession and control of the continent. These powers, as the most powerful auxiliary in securing the coveted object, sought the alliance, and aid of the Indian tribes; until the defeat of the French arms at Niagara, at Louisburg, and finally at Quebec in 1759, gave to the English, and the numerous Indian tribes with whom they were thence-forward allied, the absolute, and supreme dominion of all the lands of the continent. Sir William Johnson, as the representative of the British Monarch, obtained and exercised an unrivaled ascendency over the Indians, and during a long term of years lived in the opulent splendor, the luxurious freedom, and power that characterized the baronets of the Middle Ages. Johnson's Hall, which was the only baronial mansion ever built and sustained on American soil, being the central position of that imperial power which now ruled in unquestioned supremacy on the continent; again, this majestic and mighty Empire, the rule of the English power in America, was awaiting the arbitrament of arms here amid the quiet forests bordering on the Chemung; here the most eminent among the British leaders - Sir John Johnson, Colonel Guy Johnson, Colonel John Butler - while the haughty warriors of the Iroquois were led by their own subtle chiefs, Thayendanegea ("the Monster Brant") as well as Corn-Planter and Red Jacket - were assembled to take command, in this hour of emergency, of the combined British and Indian force, amounting to some 200 English troops, and 1,300 Iroquois, securely entrenched among the wooded hills upon the Chemung.

The American army, under command of General Sullivan, was delayed several days at Tioga in preparing for their march into the Indian territory. On August 26, the army commenced its movement in the following order of battle. Major Parr, commanding corps of riflemen, forming the advanced guard - the brigades of Generals Hand, Maxwell, and Poor, with Proctor's artillery occupying the central column, constituting the main body of the army, while General Clinton's brigade brought up the rear (see *Journal* of the expedition) and upon the first day the army marched some three miles and encamped for the night. On the succeeding day, August 27, the army resumed its march, making the distance of six miles, and then formed an encampment. On August 28, the route of the army lay through difficult mountain roads, and General Maxwell's brigade being detached for crossing the west bank of the river, the whole army marched this day only two miles.

Before the arrival of General Clinton at Tioga, General Sullivan who had reached that place on August 11, detached a small party the same evening to reconnoiter the enemy's position. This scout returned upon the succeeding day, and (quoting from Colonel Hubley's journal) with information: "made several discoveries at Chemung, an Indian village twelve miles distant from this place" and accordingly it was determined to destroy at once this prominent Indian village, and the main army commanded by General Sullivan immediately commenced its march toward Chemung, but owing to the darkness of the night did not reach this town until the next morning, August 13, but the village had been evacuated on approach of the American army by the Indians, and the army bad advanced about a mile beyond this deserted town when the vanguard discovered the enemy occupying a lofty hill upon the east bank of the Chemung River, and the American forces at once made an intrepid attack upon this position, from which, by the determined bravery of the assault, our troops soon succeeded in dislodging the Indians, who made a precipitate retreat, carrying with them their own warriors killed in this engagement, while the American army suffered a loss of seven killed, and ten wounded - the first sacrifice made by our gallant troops. The army then reduced the large Indian village of Chemung to ashes, and returned the same day to Tioga. This brilliant and successful expedition was the preliminary movement, the prelude to the final attack and overthrow of the proud Iroquois confederacy; the reverberations of our arms had startled the Acwinoshioni from his repose amid the wildwoods, the luxuriant hills, and beautiful streams, of his own empire.

Resuming the narrative of the expedition at the place where I had made interlude after referring to the termination of the march upon August 13, and encampment of our troops at Chemung on ground where the Indian village had formerly stood - the American army resumed its march, in the same order as upon the 26th, about nine o'clock on the memorable August 27, and on its "arrival near the ridge where the action of the 13th commenced" the vanguard perceived several of the enemy, who, upon approach of our forces retreated; the corps under command of Major Parr gave immediate but cautious pursuit, and proceeded "about a mile," when a large force of the subtle Indian warriors were discovered very artfully concealed behind an extensive fortification, which had been covered from view by trees and boughs being cut, and in their vernal foliage, brought and placed in an upright position in front of this redoubt. This position was admirably chosen, evincing in its selection consummate military skill and strategic art, occupying the east bank where a large bend had been formed in Chemung River, the extreme right of the entrenchment rested upon this stream, while its circuitous and rapid currents placed the rear secure from hostile surprise or approach, and the left of the redoubt rested upon a secure base of a precipitous and lofty hill - the entire work extending some half-mile in length; a beautiful island, which indeed seemed like realization of some enchanted and fairy dream of paradise, slumbered amid the waters of the Chemung within a short distance - while in the hazy sunlight the vernal magnificence of summer began to blend its sylvan hues with the crimson tints, and gorgeous yet fading colors of Autumn. General Hand immediately advanced the light corps within three hundred yards of the enemy's entrenchment; and, General Sullivan arriving upon the ground, then directed the rifle corps, under command of General Hand, to assault the enemy's works in front, while Generals Clinton's and Poor's brigades were ordered to storm and attempt to turn the left flank of the British and Indian force which was stationed upon the steep hills in that direction, and Colonel Proctor to support the attack, with artillery, while General Maxwell's was held in reserve. This skillful arrangement - these vigorous orders were promptly and bravely enforced. The light corps made a brilliant and intrepid charge upon the veteran British troops and the savage Indian warriors, who sheltered behind their formidable breastwork, as well as rocks, thickets and trees, directed an incessant fire upon our brave columns who fought with unsung passed heroism, and with varying success, and discomfiture, for two hours the Iroquois animated by brave words and fearless exertions of Brant who like a demon of evil ranged every part of the ensanguined field, held their position with unequaled obstinacy - simultaneously the enemy who occupied the lofty hill upon the extreme left fighting with determined braver), resisting the assault of the gallant legion led by Clinton and Poor, step by step, and inch by inch, and were only driven from their rocky fortresses at the point of the bayonet; the sun was sinking in the western horizon - and it seemed that approaching darkness alone could decide the terrible conflict by giving victory to the unyielding Iroquois; still from every waving, rustling thicket and shrub were unceasingly sent the unseen messengers of death upon our ranks, until it now seemed to the Americans, as erst to Macbeth that -

"Birnam wood be come to Dunsinane."

along that embattled line the American columns for a moment halted, wavered, then above their bleeding ranks, there seemed to hover, like a guardian angel, the form of absent wile, with her babe clasped to her bosom, shielding it from the murderous tomahawk - again, the heroic columns advanced with hurried step to the deadly charge, disappearing amid the fire, and smoke which enveloped all the battlefield, while our artillery dealt upon the enemy a terrific cannonade, and the martial strains of the Republic cheered our men to the fearful, impetuous charge - and along their extended, embattled lines, the British and their Indian allies, wavered; the voice of the Iroquois Chieftain Brant, then echoed over the battlefield with the despairing shout of defeat - Oonah! Oonah! and with that fatal cry the hitherto unyielding and undismayed ranks of the Iroquois warriors, and their allies, were broken, and all fled in panic and confusion. With that cry of defeat, now echoing amid their native forest, the Acwinoshioni Confederacy, which had long maintained by its powers undisputed supremacy of the continent, and held the Algonquin and Appalachian groups of the Hunter-race in subjection, was overthrown and dismembered, forever; the sovereignty, the greatness, and the power of the Iroquois departed never more to return! To the Iroquois this field was indeed a fatal Waterloo: and no other battlefield would restore to their empire its lost prestige and glory! The League of the Six Nations, which had successfully met and repulsed every invasion of their territory, defeating the powerful expeditions of Champlain in 1615, of De la Barne in 1664 - of the Marquis De Nonville in 1687, as (mentioned in *Colonial History of New York*) - and of the Count De Frontenac in 1796; and who had during the preceding years of the Revolution been the tenor of all the border settlements of our country, and whilst allied with the British had presented an invincible barrier to our military success; but here, by the waters of the Chemung which were speeding away to mingle with the ocean, and upon this quiet day as summer's regal splendor was fading and dying- the power and grandeur of the Iroquois had tied and become lost in the myths of their race, the glory of their empire had found pall and tomb and was buried forever!

    Nevertheless, this auspicious victory, so important if not indeed indispensable to the triumph of the American cause, was attained with only a comparatively small loss to the patriot army - only six were killed, and about fifty wounded. Our fallen braves were buried near the battleground.

> *"How sleep the brave who sink to rest,*
> *By all their country's wishes blest!*
> *When spring, with dewy fingers cold,*
> *Returns to deck their hallow'd mold,"*
>
> *Then honor comes, a pilgrim gray*
> *To bless the turf that wraps their clay;*
> *And Freedom shall awhile repair*
> *To dwell a weeping hermit there!*

It is known that Sir John Johnson, Brant, and indeed all the prominent leaders of the allied British and Indians in the fierce conflicts, the marvelous scenes of the Revolution, were present at the Battle of the Chemung, encouraging their followers in performance of acts of unparalleled bravery.

The Battle of the Chemung took place (as will be seen in consulting the various journals kept by officers of the expedition, and other documents) some thirteen or fourteen miles from Tioga, and seven or eight miles below Elmira. The *Journal* already quoted, mentions that the army proceeded from the encampment which it had made on the evening of August 27, after the battle, some "four miles and a half, through a mountainous country, and an almost continuous defile on east side of Cayuga branch," "then crossed Cayuga branch, where it forks with a stream running east and west," and came upon a "piece of country remarkably level," and afterwards "proceeded along the path which leads to Catharine's Town"; from this description of the march, of the situation of the various localities through which the array passed, there will now exist no difficulty in defining the position of the battle ground.

In another account of this expedition, which may be found on page 785 of Vol. VIII. of *Colonial History of New York*, it is stated that General Sullivan's action with the Indians took place at Middletown, and then gives the distance of the route traversed by the Expedition from Tioga, as follows: "12 miles to Chemung, 3 to Middletown, 9 to Newtown, 18 to Catharine's Town"; it will be remembered that the battle occurred at Middletown, which was estimated to be nine miles below Newtown, and it is well known that Catharine's Town, (which was located near the present village of Havana [now Montour Falls]) is only 18 miles from Elmira.

The fullest and most positive proof as to the precise locality of this battleground is afforded in the *Narrative* of Major Maxwell, which was written out by dictation of that prominent officer of the expedition, by General Miller and Lieutenant Allansan in 1818, and will be found included in Vol. VII, (commencing on page 97) of *Historical Collections of the Essex Institute*, and I will in this place only give a brief extract from Maxwell's *Narrative* which has reference to General Sullivan's battle with the Indians, thus:

> *"We commenced ranging over the same ground as the year before, and passed over onto the Susquehanna River, where Colonel Willet received a letter from General Sullivan, requesting him to send me to him, then near Valley Forge, to guide him to the Six Nations in the Genesee country. I went on accordingly and joined General Sullivan at Tioga Point. We started with the intention of going to Queen Catharine's Town on the south end of Seneca Lake. We went up the Chemung River to a place called Hog Back. Here the Indians ambuscaded General S., having felled a breastwork of pine timber and concealed themselves. About ten in the morning, the Six Nations attacked us. We had a severe fight, but beat the Indians and pursued them through a small Indian village to Queen Catharine's Town, and found that deserted by all save one."*

Here we thus have explicit, absolute, and unquestionable proof, afforded by one of the commanding officers of the expedition, in respect to the battle having taken place at Hog Back Hill; although, as will be observed, it directly conflicts with statements relative to locality of this battle ground, as given in several historical works. I may here mention that Major Maxwell was born in Bradford, Massachusetts, September 11, 1742; in 1757 he enlisted in the war against the French and Indians - he went with the heroic party who entered the British ships in Boston harbor and threw the tea overboard - and was engaged in the Revolutionary War from time of the first skirmish at Concord, Massachusetts on April 19, 1775, to the close of General Sullivan's campaign against the Indians; in 1800 he removed to Ohio, and participated, to some extent, in war of 1812, and he afterward resided at Detroit, Michigan, and died about the year 1830. It is mentioned in M.S. papers of Honorable Thomas Maxwell that the Battle of Chemung between General Sullivan and the Indians was fought some seven or eight miles below Elmira, at Hog Back Hill. Colonel Baldwin who was wounded in the action afterward returned and settled near the battle ground. I have also been informed by Honorable Green Bennett who now resides in this county that his father, Ephriam Bennett who was an officer in the American army in the Revolution, and soon alter the close of war removed from Warwick, Orange County, New York, to Wyoming, Pennsylvania, had in 1794 removed from Pennsylvania to the Chemung Valley, and located "his farm upon the old battle ground of Chemung at Hog's Back, where he resided until 1799 - the remains of the fortifications upon the battle field being at this period distinctly visible. My informant, Colonel Green Bennett, was a child at the time his father had lived at the place where General Sullivan fought and defeated the British and Indians. This action was popularly known as the "Battle of Newtown," but the ground where it occurred was situated about seven miles below the village of Newtown; in 1799 the Bennett family removed to Catharine's Valley. I have, too, received similar information about the battleground of Newtown being at Hog Back Hill, near Chemung or Tioga River, some miles below Elmira, from several early residents of this region who were children of Revolutionary soldiers engaged in this expedition, and had participated in the Battle of Chemung - as they respectively, had frequently heard their parents refer to the battle between Sullivan and the Indians, and the locality where it was fought. In a letter from Honorable Charles P. Avery who was the author of a valuable work about the history of this section of the State, this letter bearing date, "Flint, Michigan, June 12, 1865," it is mentioned:

> "Your favor of the 7th inst., is at hand today. The Battle of Newtown between Brant and Sullivan did not take place at Elmira, as erroneously stated by Mr. Stone in life of Brant, but at least 7 or 8 miles down the river, near a house where a Doctor Everett lived, and does now, near Hog Back Hill so called. Colonel Pickering called the Indians together at Tioga Point (Athens, Pennsylvania) and also at Newtown, Red Jacket having been present at both places, as I have always understood, and there first bringing himself into notice as an Orator. By the way, Tioga (properly Tah-hi-ho-gah) means the point of land where the streams come together-poetically, "the meeting of the waters." I have been over most of the ground mentioned by you. Make my compliments to the Historical Society of Buffalo. I appreciate and applaud their associated efforts. The members may not see their reward at once, but it will take the lapse of but a few years to make a grateful and rich return."

The views, derived from positive knowledge, upon this point about the place where the battle between Sullivan and the Indians actually occurred, of such men as Honorable Thomas Maxwell, Honorable Greene Bennett, and Judge Avery, as well as other early pioneers of the Chemung Valley, cannot fail to be conclusive. I have been thus, explicit regarding the precise locality of the battlefield of Newtown, because I have regarded it to be the province alike of the historian, as of the jurist, to give careful and exact investigation to every matter requiring attention and research, before expressing his conclusions.

It was upon a beautiful summer morning, fragrant with balm, and bloom of flowers that came wafted with every breeze, that I had passed along the picturesque, romantic shores of the Chemung River until I reached the place where the memorable battle of Newtown had been fought, and my footsteps wandered over the field where the tide of combat once rolled: I have trodden many 'battlefields of ancient and of modern fame, but as I slowly passed over this ground, by the rapid waters of the Chemung, something of the same feelings were recalled that I had known while climbing the ascent of Lundy's Lane, near the majestic Niagara - the noble, swiftly gliding river upon one side, and the steep hill upon the opposite side of the battle-ground of either of these fields of military glory, both at Chemung and at Lundy's Lane, presented nearly the same appearance. Among these hills which stretch away in hazy and indistinct outline upon the left or north bank of the river, Butler's creek takes its rise, and flowing through wild ravine and picturesque vale, unites its softly gliding waters with the Chemung at a short distance from the battlefield, while the murmuring waves of this magnificent stream breath no tale of the combat which there had transpired so long ago, upon the listening air. The fairy island is slumbering amid the currents of the river as softly in its Eden beauty as upon the long gone summer day of 1779. Upon close observation there may yet be traced some marks of the battle - the rising belt of ground stretching through the meadow land over which the tall, luxuriant grass is now growing, along the line where the fortifications had once extended from the banks of the river until it intersected with the rugged hills on its western side. A large and ancient cucumber tree is still standing upon the eastern part of the field, it had once sheltered the combatants who fought beneath its ample foliage, and the remains of the old apple tree are yet here. Near the spot where it had grown, Colonel Baldwin had fallen severely wounded in the battle on August 29, 1779, and the orchard that he had set out after his removal here is still remaining near the battleground. The field was divided by a rail fence, and upon one side cattle and sheep were grazing:

"The situation seems stall formed for fame,
A hundred thousand men might fight again
With ease. But, where sought for Elion's walls.
The quiet sheep feeds, and the tortoise crawls."

I will return to the narrative of General Sullivan's expedition. Upon the day succeeding the Battle of Newtown, in an address that General Sullivan issued to the army, consequently of the neglect of the Board of War to supply the expedition with adequate means of transportation, military stores, provisions, and forage, he was obliged to propose, in order move completely to accomplish the important objects of the campaign, that the troops should accept half rations, referring in this address, to the reasons which dictated such a measure, and the patriotic and heroic army unanimously expressed their concern with this proposition. On August 31, as previously referred to, the army commenced its march. Crossing the Cayuga branch where it formed a junction with another stream which flowed from the west, where they destroyed an Indian village, Newtown (the present city of Elmira) the army then pursued its march until reaching the "'Town of the Indian Queen, Catherine Montour," where it arrived September 1. The army reached Kanadaseaga (now Geneva, New York) the Indian Castle at the foot of Seneca Lake, which was immediately burned, on September 7. In the progress of the invasion, the army arrived at Canandaigua, situated near the lake bearing the same name, on September 10, and destroyed the town, and then Honeoye, New York, which was burned. General Sullivan, without making any pause, proceeded to the rich valley of the Genesee river, where the principal capital of the Senecas, Genesee, was located in a fertile region, whose orchards and fields of waving grain, not less than its hamlets and villages, indicated the civilization of many centuries. This large town was destroyed. On September 15, the army having accomplished the essential objects of the expedition, received orders of General Sullivan, to recommence its march for Tioga. Consequently, of the insufficient supply of stores, General Sullivan being compelled to return without proceeding to Niagara, and in retracing the path of the victorious expedition the army reached the valley of Catharine's Creek about September, 24 and owing to the entire failure of forage for horses of the cavalry force, several hundred horses were obliged to be killed, and the place where this was done has since retained the name of Horseheads, New York.

The army arrived at the original rendezvous, at Tioga, upon September 30, and the main army, under command of General Sullivan, reached Wilkes-Barre on October 7, having commenced the invading march on the preceding July 31, 1779, and within the intervening period of two months and seven days, this army had signally defeated the allied British and Indians within their own entrenchments at Chemung, desolated the country of the hitherto invincible Iroquois, and burned over forty of their village, caving but a wreck of their once proud domain. Nevertheless, for the reason that General Sullivan, in his address to the army, had referred in just terms of censure to the action of the Board of War in withholding supplies from the expedition, this gallant General was permitted to retire from the service, although the sagacious statesman, and inflexible patriot, Elbridge Gerey, made an effort in Congress to have General Sullivan retained in command, it was ineffectual. General Sullivan afterwards was elected to Congress, and held various important positions in the State of New Hampshire, and his decease occurred January 23, 1795.

    It is mentioned in the elaborate *History of the Indian Tribes*, by H. R. Schoolcraft, (page 310, Vol. VI) in reference to the Battle of Chemung. "This battle decided the results of the campaign; and, as Aboriginal history proves, it effectually destroyed the Iroquois confederacy." However, during the ensuing year bands of Indian warriors continued frequently to make incursions upon our frontier settlements. In allusion to these massacres which still with their recital thrill our veins with horror, J. R. Kimms, Esq., the talented author of an interesting work, *History of Schoharie County, etc.*, in a communication dated, "Fort Plain, New York, April 28, 1865," thus writes me:

> "The expedition of Sullivan which laid desolate the Indian settlements of Western New York, was rolled back the next season, by the Indians and Tories in fire and blood, on the Pioneer white settlements of the Schoharie and Mohawk valleys, during which season Brant made for himself such a reputation, that his very name carried terror to the fireside of every exposed settler."

Nevertheless, this important episode in the history of the valley, the expedition of General Sullivan, has already long claimed our attention - and I will now dismiss the subject.

CHAPTER V

Early History the region of the Susquehanna adjoining Chemung Valley - The ancient Indian village of Onaquaga. The early settlement of Owego &c. Reminiscences of Binghamton; the late Honorable D. S. Dickinson. Early annals of the region lying near headwaters of the Susquehanna - Washington's visit in 1783 – Cooperstown - J. Fennimore Cooper

Farther along this picturesque valley, or rather in adjacent valley of the Susquehanna, the famous Indian town, Onaquaga (now Windsor, New York) is situated in a romantic vale, some fourteen miles from the present town of Binghamton, New York. A mission had been established at Onaquaga, at the instance of Preston Edwards, and was placed under charge of Reverend Gideon Hawley as early as 1754. This ancient village had been the capital of a powerful Indian nation during the lapse of an immemorial period, and had held an important position in the early wars of the French and English, numerous expeditions being fitted and sent out upon their hostile errands from this castle. It had also formed, during several preceding centuries, a resting place in the excursions and journeys of the Six Nations to the Indian tribes inhabiting the banks of the Delaware, and other portions of the Southern country; while it became the headquarters of Brant in the fearful border wars of 1777-79, where this chief had organized the bands of Indian warriors which desolated the frontier settlements - this renowned Indian castle, indeed, had held an important and prominent place during all our Colonial and Revolutionary history. A party of emigrants from Connecticut settled Windsor in 1785. In 1786, James McMaster, William McMaster, Amos Draper, from Wyoming County [Pennsylvania], and by other emigrants from Massachusetts and Connecticut, commenced a settlement at Owego, New York. Near the village of Owego, in a picturesque and rural spot upon the banks of Owego Creek, Glen Mary was situated - this pleasant residence had been the home of the distinguished and lamented poet N. P. Willis, at the time his beautiful *Rural Letters* were written, and the romantic scenery of this enchanting region had furnished requisite inspiration for his genius, his rare and exquisite descriptive powers; - while I write, the melancholy intelligence comes that the immortal Poet has passed to his quiet rest, but above his grave spring will scatter its fairest and most fragrant flowers, and summer birds there will sing their sweetest melodies- forever, with their balm and their music lulling the death-slumbers of our country's deeply mourned, gifted singer. Tioga County was taken from Montgomery County and organized as a separate county on February 16, 1791; or rather, by the organic act, it was constituted a half-shire county, and the courts were held alternately at Newtown Point (now Elmira) and at Chenango (now Binghamton) in 1806, the half-shire was discontinued upon organization of Broome County in 1812, the county seat was removed from Elmira to Spencer; in 1822, by act of the Legislature, the half-shire was reestablished and the courts were held at Elmira and Owego; and on erection of Chenango County, in 1836 from limits of Tioga, Elmira became the county seat of Chemung County and Owego was designated as the county seat of Tioga.

Binghamton, which is located in one of the richest and most delightful sections of the Susquehanna Valley, still farther toward the source of the majestic stream which gives the tribute of beauty and verdure to the romantic shores that border its noble waters, was settled it an early date; its pioneer, Captain Joseph Leonard, having moved, with his family, up the Susquehanna in a canoe from Wyoming, and settled here in 1787. Colonel William Rose, and other emigrants, mostly from New England, also made settlement at this place about the same period. The village is pleasantly located upon the north side of the Susquehanna, at its junction with the Chenango River - and the place was first designated by name of Chenango Point. The Reverend Mr. Howe, of the Baptist persuasion, had conducted in 1788 the earliest religious exercises within this town. Broome County was organized in 1806, and Binghamton became the county seat - the first court in the new county was held in May 1806, John Patterson being the first judge. Binghamton will derive its principal distinction, however, in the records of history as having been the home of the late Honorable D. S. Dickinson, who had earned a brilliant, not less than well merited pre-eminence as a learned and astute lawyer, a wise and patriotic statesman. He was deputed to represent New York in the U. S. Senate - at the auspicious time when its councils were ruled by the mastermind of Dallas who had won enduring fame as one of the ablest among the distinguished public men in the better days of the Republic - and at the memorable period which this august body was composed of the most eminent statesmen and brilliant orators of our land, whose matchless eloquence had so often achieved enduring triumph in this proud forum of debate. Within the American Senate yet, I may only recall the honored names of the illustrious Thomas H. Benton who had occupied for a longer period of years than any other public man of our nation a place in this august forum, and had here established preeminent fame not only as the *Princeps Senatus* of the legislative councils of the Republic, but also as the ablest and wisest statesman of our land and in regard to him. I may well adopt the sentiment of the great drama in the words of Mark Antony applied to Brutus:

"This was the noblest Roman of them all;
His life was gentle, and the elements
So mixed in him, that nature might stand up,
And say to all the world - This was a man"

together with the eminent names of the imperious Webster, of the astute Calhoun, of the eloquent Clay, of the learned Berrian, of the laborious Cass, of the accomplished Woodbury, and of the brilliant and scholastic Clayton, whom I now can name only to deplore; and here at this epoch, mingling in the debates and councils of the Senate, were then the able and eminent senator from Pennsylvania, Honorable James Buchanan, and who had afterward occupied the important positions, of Secretary of State, and of Chief Magistrate of the Union, preceding his retirement to private life- and the Honorable Reverend Johnson of Maryland who had long held distinguished rank among the accomplished statesmen of the better days of the Republic, and still remains, in the plenitude of his power and fame within the Senate, while he is acknowledged to be, not only as one of the roost learned and astute jurists of our country, but as pre-eminently the ablest, most eloquent and illustrious Statesman now holding a place in the Public Councils of the Nation. Clay and Calhoun, soon after leaving their places in the Senate, reposed within their honored graves, covered with flowers born of a southern sun, and wakened to bud and to bloom by the balmy airs of the tropics - and the great orator and Statesman of New England, Webster,

"Broken with the storms of State," had too soon passed to rest in the lowly tomb. Mr. Dickinson, I believe, had first entered the Senate at its session of 1844-45; it was indeed a brilliant epoch, resplendent with the first glories of the Republic. Great measures that would give the enduring impress to the policy of our government required adjustment, and in their discussion he evinced the giant grasp of mind, the massive strength of judgment, the great argumentative power, which then began to show the colossal proportion of his intellect, and gave such promise at the commencement of his senatorial career, *primis oninibus*, of its effulgent splendor; and in the noblest qualities that go to form the judicious legislator, or in the expressive words of Cicero, the "bonus Senatoris prudential," Mr. Dickinson was indeed entitled to rank as the peer of the great and most illustrious statesmen of the Republic.

In the early part of 1860, when the larger portion of our public men treated any danger of a disruption of the harmonious relations of the several states only as an illusion of the fancy, Mr. Dickinson had regarded with most painful apprehension the unhappy political condition of our country; and when treason dually sought to accomplish its criminal designs through the instrumentality of armed force, he was still found, as he had been of yore, devoting every energy in sustaining the Constitution and the Union, always remembering that *vigilantia aeterna liberatis pretium est*. From the personal relations which the writer of this sketch had been privileged to enjoy for many years with Honorable D. S. Dickinson, I can truly say, that he was always sincere and earnest in his adherence to political principles, not less than inflexible in their maintenance, *vir justus, et tenax proposite*; and his life was marked by profound and unwavering patriotism, a refined and elevated sense of honor, rare and unswerving integrity, and wisdom which was enriched by the ample stores of experience:

> *"A combination and a form indeed*
> *Where every God did seem to set his seal*
> *To give the world assurance of a man."*

But, the summons came to call him away, at a period, indeed, of life when he had gathered the amplest public honors; nor medical skill, nor assiduity of friends had power to revive or restore him - had no longer any power to resume the wanting fire of life whose brilliancy lingering even to its earthly close. Another great statesman has thus gone down to the dust; the tomb contains all that is left of him whose name had become known throughout the earth. Well may we pause; he, whose counsels had guided us so long, will be with us no more forever. In the quietness of the political atmosphere we are startled by the death notes, which at intervals are sounded as from the trumpet of the Archangel to call an entire people to mourning, and the nation is overshadowed in gloom as in the darkness of the sun's eclipse. The luminary which has shed its benign light in the noon-day heavens, while a still brighter effulgence had crowned its calm setting with a mild and sweet farewell - allowing a brief yet beautiful repose ere the coming of the eternal night- has passed from our horizon. but leaving its lingering radiance to show that it has not quenched its orb, but shines in the firmament forever! He belongs to the immortal galaxy - Thompkins, Wright, Dickinson - now complete; which takes its place amid the loftier constellations, ante alias ignes astrorum, and giving its light unto the heavens! He indeed is gone; but his name will live when the millions that moved around him are forgotten. The old Republics are in ruins; the grass now grows amid the Areopagus and in the Forum, but the names of Demosthenes and Cicero survive, though the places where they rest are now unknown and, that name, also, which has been repeated around every hearthstone of the new Republic, too, shall endure when perchance the Republic itself has been swept away, and the men of future times come and search in vain for the relics of our glory and of our grandeur. His honored name, at least, cherished by the remembrance of personal kindness, the recollection of long years of uninterrupted friendship, will not be forgotten by him who pays this humble and imperfect tribute to his illustrious memory.

It is indeed humiliating, when we recall to mind the elevated and eminent position which had been so brilliantly acquired, and so long and amply sustained by the American Senate, and whereto in the balmiest days of its renown. New York had then deputed such very able and pre-eminent statesmen as Rufus King, Van Buren, Wright, Marcy, Dickinson; and then to give, today (February 1867) a moment's reflection upon the very common - place character of this deliberative body, as it is now constituted, and which particularly marks the present Senatorial delegation from New York, and the representation, with few exceptions, in the popular branch of the American Congress. Again, we cross the rotunda, and enter the senate chamber – it was at the memorable session of 1849-50, but a short time before the expiration of Mr. Dickinson's senatorial term; the eminent Vice President rules the stormy debates of this Amphictyonic Council of the Republic- the shades of mighty statesmen glide along the majestic aisles, and the eloquent voices of the past echo amid the corridors and colonnades of the senate chamber; in its proud forum, where now were assemble the illustrious Statesmen who so had shaped the destinies of the Republic, meeting here for the last time on earth - the senior Senator of New York eloquently urged the adoption of the series of measures, to which the entire country then were looking as the only relief for political and sectional disquietudes, earnestly hoping that with their success would dawn a more effulgent morn, a fairer season in the progress of our Republic:

"The winter of our discontent
Made glorious summer by this sun of York"

With the close of this Congress, Mr. Dickinson, with other distinguished statesmen who were among his compeers in the Senate, bade final adieu to this theatre of lofty triumph, but once the days of the Conscript Father's none unobtrusively greater have sat within the Council Halls of the Republic. Again, after the lapse of seventeen years, we enter the vestibule, and pass along this imposing aisle of the senate chamber, but the Master-Statesmen of the Republic who once guided its Legislative councils have passed away forever, the voices which had so long charmed the listening Senate are hushed and still, and the unrivaled glory which lingered around this august forum, and clustered amid the graceful arches, and lofty galleries of Senate chamber, too, has vanished like Prospero's dream. But, the murmur of this noble river interrupts our musing - and I must bid farewell to this classic ground which had so long been the home of the statesman of the Susquehanna.

The majestic Susquehanna, which in its loveliness and grandeur is gliding by, whispers enchanting tales of the romantic, picturesque scenery which continues to border its murmuring waters, and which surrounds the mountain springs whose crystal fountains first give shape to the tributary streams of this magnificent river - and lulled by its music, I, too, am lured by its beauty to ascend still further along the lovely, fairy shores of the Susquehanna until I shall reach its source. Around this region cluster the rich historic associations of the past- and around the sylvan lake whose tranquil waters feed the beautiful Susquehanna, linger the proudest reminiscences connected with the literature of our land, whose luster will ever remain in its unfading and immortal glory.

Already, as I leisurely glide along the waters of the Susquehanna, I have passed the boundaries of Broome and enter the limits of

Chenango County. This county includes several "Twenty Towns" which the Indians, in a Treaty held at Fort Schuyler in 1788 with Governor George Clinton, had deeded to the State, and which was known as "Clinton's Purchase." Settlements had been made upon the Susquehanna River, within the present towns of Afton and Bainbridge, New York, in 1785 and 1786, by emigrants from Vermont and Connecticut. Mr. S. Ketchum had made the pioneer settlement of Greene in 1712, and in the same year, a party of French refugees located within this town, and made purchase of a tract amounting to 15,000 acres lying upon Chenango River. The distinguished diplomat, Talleyrand, visited his countrymen at this place in 1794, but owing to some defect in the title of lands purchased by this early French colony, the settlement was abandoned in 1796. Among other early settlers in Greene, and who remained permanently in this section, were Reverend Nathan Kellogg who about 1795, organized the earliest church (Baptist) within this county, and continued as its pastor for a period of 30 years; and Mr. B. Loomis, C. Hill, D. Tremain, resettled in East Greene in 1798. The Honorable George A. S. Crooker who in former years has held the first rank among the most eloquent, persuasive orators, the most brilliant and successful lawyers in western New York - and long occupied a distinguished position, and in the Constitutional Convention of 1846 - had passed his boyhood days in this picturesque region; and, in re-visiting his early home in the year 1850, had written one of his most beautiful poems in which he recalls the cherished associations which clustered around the romantic hills of "worshiped Greene" - in this exquisite poem, occurs the sweet and plaintive allusion to the loved one of life's young hours, and which in pathos and beauty of sentiment has been rarely excelled:

"Affections' young flower.
That budded to blossom in beauty and pride,
Has wasted its sweetness, and withered and died;
Her spirit in dreams to my pillow bath come-
When far in the wild-woods, to beckon me home."

I may be allowed to add in this place that the life or personal career of the talented poet whose felicitous imagery has been embodied in many passages similar to the one above quoted, in the dramatic and impassioned series of romances connected with it - as the writer of this sketch has had opportunity to be aware - would form a story of far wilder, and more intense interest than the pen of the novelist has ever been permitted to record. But, the celestial fire that had burnt so early, and so brightly, is now growing dim- its light and warmth now waning; the sere and mildew are now fast gathering over the eloquent chords of his harp that soon will slumber in silence forever. Amid the shadows which linger over his beautiful melodies, a fair *Ariel* even hovers, to scatter with noiseless wing bright rays of light - and amid the notes of sadness, the bird of paradise ever returns to warble its native strains, and to bring fresh flowers from Elysian groves of immortal fragrance and beauty. When once within the mazes of his poetry, you then seem to be wandering in some fairy land - of sunny groves, and bright streams, where the moonlight falls in gorgeous showers, where music ever murmurs its soft melodies, and the fragrant breath of summer flowers laden the balmy zephyrs - yet with all this beauty tinged by the melancholy hues of twilight. Indeed, in his numbers can be traced the noblest qualities of the Divine Art; a fancy brilliant and glowing, which like the sunlight illuminates every object its rays may touch, and transforms it into some image of beauty - and

"Doth suffer a sea change into something rich and strange."

But, there is another, and more lasting charm that holds you spellbound; - it is the sympathetic, wondrous power of awakening with intensest emotion the feelings which lie enshrined in the inmost recesses of the bosom, with the melancholy strains of sadness, as the poet wanders back to revel in the fair dreamland of days that come no more, murmurs in mournful sweetness along the chords of his harp - which indeed seem like snatches of some divine melody, chanted upon Seraph's lyre, and which but breathes response to the low, deep undertone ever thrilling the human heart. I might well hope that the many beautiful poems written by Mr. Crooker should be carefully gathered and published in a style commensurate with their worth; and thus, when his harp becomes forever silent, and perchance the work of more ostentatious poets are forgotten and lost, posterity may turn with admiration and delight, to his soothing, heartfelt melodies. It has been remarked, that there is not a stream in the land beyond the ocean but whose praises have been sung - and who, indeed, has not heard the voice that murmurs from the Arno, from Avor, from Ayre, from Leman's Lake and the River Po - and the romantic stream gliding in beauty and music amid these quiet hills and vales of Greene, had first kindled by their poetic associations, the imagination, and inspired the muse of the gifted poet who in after years had so eloquently described their loveliness in the flowing numbers of song. I have thus dwelt, at some length, upon the genius of one of the most brilliant orators and poets of our land. The first poem which I remember of listening, read to me in days of early childhood, had been written by the poet to whom I have above referred; and afterward, my earliest poetical reading, which included *Childe Harold,* had been pursued within his library - then little dreaming that I should ever recall the historical reminiscences of the beautiful region where his childhood and boyhood years had been passed.

Chenango County was organized in 1778 - and included towns which were taken from Herkimer and Tioga Counties. The new county was first formed with half-shires, the courts being held at Hamilton (now within Madison County which had been erected in 1806) and at Oxford. In accordance with a Legislative Act on March 6, 1807, Norwich was designated as the county seat of Chenango, and the courthouse - a wooden structure, was built in 1809, in which the courts held their sessions until about 1837, when a new courthouse, constructed of brick, was erected here. Among the early county officers, I may name Isaac Foote, first judge, J. Enos and J. Leland, associate Judges, and William Tracy, Sheriff - who held their offices from the time of organization of the County during several subsequent years.

Within Chenango County, at various places, had formerly existed the interesting, mysterious monuments reared by that vast, and powerful empire that once held dominion of our soil. In the town of Oxford, situated upon the banks of the Chenango River, there had been an ancient enclosure, which occupied a small eminence. The shore descended from this elevation precipitously to the stream, whilst upon the hill, an embankment, some four feet in height, with a trench upon the outside of the elevated mound, extended in a semicircular form, and enclosing in the fortification about three-fourths of an acre of ground. A pine tree, apparently of three or four hundred years in growth, stood upon this ancient work. The Indians had a tradition that this fort had been occupied by their ancestors reaching back to the seventh generation - but relative to the origin of the fortification, they were entirely unacquainted. The remains of an old fortification, which at the time of the early French & Indian wars, was known as "the castle," are located in the town of Norwich. These earthworks had been examined, many years since, by DeWitt Clinton. Within the town of Greene, some two miles from the village, and situated near the Chenango River, there had formerly existed a mound of the most interesting character.

This tumulus had an elevation of some six feet and diameter of about forty feet; and upon excavation being made in 1829, several human skeletons were first disclosed, and beneath this layer, were found a deposit of human bones which had been burned - presenting only the charred ostelogical remains, and, in this respect showing the same characteristic feature which marks the mound-period of the Mississippi Valley. In this mound also were discovered several interesting, and rare relics of art; among them a silver bracelet, a plate of mica, cut or fashioned in ornamental shape, stone chisels, beside several hundred arrowheads, &c. In the year 1811, there had been found in Norwich, a nearly entire specimen of Indian pottery; this was a vessel something shaped like a jar with its upper portion in an oval or rounded form, and with a groove molded in the vessel near its upper rim, and holding in capacity, some three quarts. This relic hid been figured and described in the *New York Medical and Philosophical Register* for 1812. I have thus been able to notice only a, few of the ancient works, and artistic remains, which the Mound-builders had left in this county - and which would show in after times some record of their power and their greatness.

In pursuing our way still farther along the Susquehanna Valley, I can delay only for a short time in recalling some incidents connected with the history of Delaware County, which here borders upon the southern side of the river. The first town in the county that I reach in ascending the Susquehanna, which was organized in 1801 as Sidney, New York, had been explored at the early period of 1772 by Reverend William Johnston who came and settled with his family upon the present site of Sidney

Plains in the ensuing year - thus commencing the first settlement made in the Susquehanna Valley within the limits of New York State. It was at this place, within a brief period before the commencement of the war of the Revolution that General Herkimer held an interview with Thayendanegea (the Mohawk Chief Brant.)

The remains of an Indian Fortification, now known as "the Fort Grounds," which included some three acres, and was surrounded by a low parapet of earth, and a valum or ditch, are located in this town, near the place where the first settlement by civilized man had been made within the Susquehanna Valley. A settlement was made at Harpersfield, New York, now in Delaware County, in 1771, by Colonel John Harper. The settlement here was destroyed in April 1780, by a party of Tories and Indians; and during this raid, Captain Alexander Harper, and several other pioneer settlers who were with him at the time, were captured and carried to Niagara - while three of his associates were massacred at once by the Indians. At Niagara, Captain Harper met with some relatives who had been taken prisoners in 1778 at Cherry Valley; and all remained in captivity until the triumph of the American cause," and restoration of peace in 1783, effected their release, and allowed them to return, after this long and painful absence, to their homes. The early settlement at Harpersfield, however, had been abandoned consequent to the hostile raids in the border-warfare of the Revolution. In 1784, Colonel John Harper, with his sons William, Alexander, and Joseph Harper who were all eminent and active patriots in the Revolutionary struggle, returned and made a permanent settlement al Harpersfield. Delaware County embraces a part of the original Hardenburg Patent, which had been granted in 1708, and which had been principally surveyed in the year 1749, by E. Wooster. In 1768, John Harper and his associates bought of the Indians, at Johnson Hall, Montgomery County, a tract of 250,000 acres. The larger portion of this county, or the most part of the lands it contained, was settled upon leases that are an incongruous element in our Republican system, as it is an unhappy relic of the medieval ages. This feudal system, too, had produced a conflict a few years since within the borders of Delaware County, and several other portions of our state, which may be compared to the wars of the old barons who gathering their forces within their moated strongholds, their Castles with battlement and turret, fought to maintain the dominion over all their broad lands. In 1844-1845, many citizens of Delaware County, whenever the civil officers undertook to levy for rent, also assembled in large numbers, organized into armed bands, and acting under command of an elected chief, and who in name &c., assumed the character of the Indian Sachem, for resisting the enforcement of these writs. This contest with alternate success and defeat, continued for some months, between the civil officers, and the organized parties that boldly resisted the execution of the writs, denying the authority and defying the power of the Sheriff; during this conflict. Deputy Sheriff Steele was killed in the town of Andes, New York; and the excitement that reigned so intensely and supremely in Delaware County, also largely pervaded other sections of the State, and excited an important influence then in shaping the political history of New York - Delaware County was formed, March 10, 1797 from Ulster and Otsego Counties. Delhi is the county seat. The first courthouse was built about the year 1798, which was afterward burned, and another courthouse was erected in 1820; the first county officers were J. H. Brett, first judge P. Lamb, G. North, and W. Horton, judges. At the early period when a portion of the territory now included in this county was attached to Ulster, the State Convention of New York held its session within the limits of the county as then existing - the Convention Meeting at Kingston - and then in 1775, framed the earliest State Constitution of New York, and which continued in force with addition of several amendments, until 1823. This Constitution embraced wise and comprehensive principles of Constitutional Law, but it added no new feature to our political system, and gave no new right to the citizens, but it constituted "simply a re-affirmation of the liberties enjoyed prior to the American Revolution, and which had previously been asserted in the "Great Charter," (*Magna Charta*) of 1215 - in the "Confirmatio Chartarum" of 1297- in the "Statue of Treasons" of 1350 - in the "Petition of Right" of 1627 - in the "Habeas Corpus Act" of 1679 in the "Bill of Rights" of 1689 of the "Body of Liberties" of 1641 -in the "Articles of Confederation of the United Colonies of New England" of 1643 and finally, in the "Declaration of Independence" of 1776. This place, Kingston, being the Capital of the State when Sir Henry Clinton acquired possession of the parts in the Hudson Highlands, it was marked by the British general for destruction; and accordingly a squadron of light frigates, containing some 3,600 men, was dispatched on this expedition, and effecting a landing at Kingston Point, New York on October 13, 1777, the troops proceeded immediately to Kingston, then containing nearly four thousand inhabitants, and wantonly reduced the village to ashes. This, and other raids of similar character made in Ulster County, fully aroused its citizens in behalf of the cause of Independence. Many instructing episodes in the Colonial and Revolutionary history of this region, which bordering upon the noble Susquehanna stretches away until it becomes lost in the azure haze of the distant Catskill Mountains, are elaborately traced in the several volumes of *Collections of the Ulster Historical Society*, and in other historical works.

    I have thus given an outline of some of the more important events that had occurred in the region bordering upon the east bank of the Susquehanna, and which as the border-warfare of the Revolution extended throughout all the country whose annals I have designed to record, is inseparably interwoven with the early history of the Chemung Valley. These events, which had been enacted either in the region lying east of the Susquehanna river and stretching away towards the waters of the Hudson, or among the hills and valleys that border the west bank of the Susquehanna whose thrilling episodes I now narrate, with the story of the expedition whose conquering path led through the Chemung and Seneca Lake valleys in 1779, all belong to a single act connected with the great drama of the Revolutionary struggle - and cannot be separated; or rather, a single scene - and which cannot be obscured, or obliterated without injuring or destroying the whole. I have earlier made an allusion to the interesting reminiscences connected with Oquago, the ancient capitol of the Mohawk Indians; and have also traced the early annals of other places in the Susquehanna Valley within the present limits of Tioga, Broome, and Chenango counties.

Unadilla, New York, which is situated on the Susquehanna in the southern part of Otsego County - the Unadilla River forming its western boundary - had held an important place in our Revolutionary history. Several families had located in this town before the Revolution, these pioneer settlements then forming the farthest advances in the westward progress of civilization. Among the most cherished and hallowed recollections of the writer of this sketch are those, which wandering back to the fairy realm of childhood's reminiscences, cling around the name of Unadilla - and are associated with the border legends of Otsego. Most indelibly impressed in memory, the writer often recalls to mind those pleasant evenings in his earliest childhood when he would sit by the blazing fireside, and listen to the wondrous stories which his grandparent who had been among the early settlers of Unadilla, related of the hardy adventures, and the daring achievements which characterized the first settlement, particularly during period of the border warfare with the Indians, in the region of Otsego; and the breathless interest which I had then, between the age of three and six years, listened to those stirring legends of the past, has ever held its influence, fresh and glowing, and retained its impression, upon the deepest and most sacred tablets of my memory. This has been, indeed, one of the strongest inclinations that prevailed in inducing me to wander over this memorable ground for retracing its scenes of historic interest. The narrator of these tales of the border, Mr. Willard Cheney, had been actively engaged in the early French and Indian wars, as also in the Revolution, and he was conversant with the incidents that still throw an absorbing interest around the early history of Tryon County. I had learned from the reminiscences thus related to me in early days of childhood that Unadilla had been first settled about the period of the last French and Indian war, or soon after its close, by emigrants from Salem (now within the limits of Washington County); some time afterward General Martin, Mr. Beach, &c, made settlement at this place, Mr. S. Crooker (father of Honorable George A. S. Crooker, earlier referred to in this sketch) some years subsequent to the Revolutionary War removed to this town, and built the first grist mill here, and in connection with the mill constructed a dam across the Susquehanna River, which causing much inconvenience to the settler residing in the valley above, they rallied in considerable excitement and forcibly removed the dam. It was also related, among many other incidents told in respect to pioneer history of the region of the Susquehanna, that the earliest settler in Otsego County, soon after he had selected his home in the wilderness, and had only just began to clear away the primitive forest and to teach the virgin soil to yield its fruits, and having filled to store sufficient provisions for the winter which proved to be of unusual inclemency, and a great depth of snow had filled and completely obstructed the path to the nearest settlements on the Mohawk River, a lingering death by starvation seemed unavoidable, when a friendly Indian who had traversed the wastes of snow by means of snow-shoes, providentially came to the house of the suffering pioneer, and upon learning his pitiful situation, at once went to the settlement on the Mohawk and obtained provisions, which, carrying upon his shoulders, he returned across the drifted snows to the abode of the famishing settler, and in this manner repeatedly supplied throughout the long and dreary winter the family of the pioneer with provisions - and thus this untutored child of nature.

"Unknown to fortune and to fame,"

by these acts of noble and generous friendship, and I may truly add, of Christian heroism, was instrumental in preserving the lives of the earliest inhabitants in Otsego County. The wild legends, which had thrilled my nerves with their recital, connected with the terrible Indian raids at Cherry Valley and other exposed settlements of the border, which were instigated and led by Brant, I remember we were also told in the days of "long ago," within that little, wood-colored, and vine-bowered cottage, which stood near the waters of the dark and gloomy Conewango, and to my childish fancy these border-scenes comprised about all the history of the world. In returning to gather reminiscences of Otsego, I feel something of the pleasure which thrills the wanderer's bosom as his eye again meets the long lost, but once familiar and deeply loved scenes of his childhood. The principal narrator of these stirring events who thus taught my earliest lessons in history. Mr. Willard Cheney, was well acquainted with General Herkimer and with General Schuyler, and spoke of both officers in terms of warmest commendation and praise. This early resident amid the wilds of Otsego, Mr. Willard Cheney, removed to Chautauqua County in 1816, where he assisted in forming the pioneer settlement in the town among whose wildwoods he had selected his home in the evening of life - his decease occurring in 1844; and I may add that he traced the history of his ancestry in this country back to the landing of Mayflower. Many episodes in his personal history, though of strange interest in themself, but not interlinked in the chain of historic events of public character which had transpired in Otsego, then Tryon County, I shall omit to mention- only narrating events of general interest.

  The idea has been entertained by several scholars, and learned historical writers, that the renowned Spanish navigator, De Soto, whom It is claimed had made discovery of the Floridas in the early part of the sixteenth century had also made an excursion into central New York. The historian of the adventures of De Soto relates that as the Spanish conqueror was conducting an expedition into the interior of America, far north of the Floridas, they had reached a place, in the neighborhood of a beautiful lake, and this locality possessed a very cold climate. This was called by the natives "Sakima'ing," which has been supposed to have same meaning or apply to some place as the Susquehanna (as these words, spoken in the Indian dialect, would sound very nearly alike) - and that, De Soto, about 1530, had actually explored the region of the Susquehanna. This suggestion, however, rests upon much too uncertain foundation, is much too vague, to he admitted as a historical fact.

  In 1701, the Unadilla River (or Tienaderha) was visited by Captain J. Blurker and Mr. D. Schuyler, while these gentlemen were pursuing a journey to "Onondaga" for arranging, in behalf of the commissioners at Albany, an important negotiation with the Five Nations; and the account of their visit to the region of the Unadilla, is given in their *Journal*, and is included, in pages 880, 890, Vol. IV, *Colonial History of New York*. I find no other authentic records about the region of the Unadilla for a long period subsequently. In October 1768, at a treaty held with the Six Nations, at Fort Stanwix, a tract of 100,000 acres of land, lying between the Unadilla River and Otsego Lake was purchased of the Indians. This purchase was affected by Colonel George Crogan, and for the extensive tract of land he obtained a patent in the succeeding year 1709, when he also secured in addition to 18,000 acres situated in Cherry Valley. Colonel Crogan was a native of Ireland. He had emigrated to America, and first settled at Pennsboro on the Susquehanna river in Pennsylvania. About 1746, he was a trader among the Indians, and in this capacity traversed the shores of Lake Erie, now included in Ohio; he was commissioned as Captain in Braddock's Expedition of 1755, and in 1756 he repaired to Sir. W. Johnson, whom he accompanied to Onondaga, and in same year Colonel Crogan received appointment as Deputy Indian Agent. (See Pennsylvania Archives, Vol. 1,742, *Penn Colonial Records* V. 139, "Archives" 11,089, & etc.,).

At this treaty, the Indians had made the proposal that the Unadilla River should form, a portion of the boundary line to be established between the English and the Indians. This line was ratified in the treaty then concluded, and is marked by a red line in the map drawn by Guy Johnson, a copy of which is in VIII Vol. of *Colonial Documents*.

In June 1777, Brant, who had during some months previous remained with a large party of Indians at Oquago, came to Unadilla, and sent a message expressing his wish to see the Reverend William Johnston, (who several years before had succeeded in establishing a flourishing settlement upon the east side of the Susquehanna,) and other prominent patriots of that section; and, upon their arrival, the Mohawk chief very coolly informed them that the Indians were in need of provisions, and if they were not furnished by consent of the inhabitants, the Indian party under his command, some 80 warriors, should take the requisite amount by force. The early pioneers of the Unadilla Country then brought in some provisions, and Brant, with his party, after remaining two days at this place, returned, taking along with them cattle, sheep, provisions, &c. The inhabitants of this region, who had espoused the cause of Independence, at once removed with their families to places that were considered more secure from Indian attacks. In July, General Herkimer, having learned of this incursion of Brant and his followers, marched with a force of 380 militia to Unadilla. The American general was met at this place by Brant at the head of 130 warriors. At this meeting, Brant recounted the grievances of which the Indians complained against the Americans, and expressed substantially his determination to act with the adherents of the British king in the war that was then being waged against the patriots. One of General Herkimer's men. Colonel Cox, then remarked, that if such was the purpose of the Iroquois, nothing further could be arranged. The wily Mohawk chief then addressed a few words to his warriors, and immediately they raised a loud shout, and ran to their camp, where, seizing their arms, a number of volleys were fired, and they then gave the terrific Indian war-whoop, and again repaired to the place where Brant and the American general had been holding their conference. General Herkimer now said to the Indian chief that the Americans had not come for fighting. Brant, whose object in producing the threatening movement by his followers had doubtless been to intimidate the American party, gave the signal for the Indians to be quiet, but assuming a hostile attitude himself, lie then demanded of the American general acquiescence in several matters, which General Herkimer was willing to allow upon condition that the Indians should not harbor the Tories and deserters, that such person should be surrendered to the Americans. Brant refused to accede to this proposition, and said that he would go to Oswego and join Butler. General Herkimer had sufficient force to have attacked and completely defeated the party under command of Brant, but the American general appears to have entertained some hope that the Iroquois might be induced, at some future time, to relinquish their intention of joining the British in prosecuting this war.

This conference at Unadilla, nevertheless, appears to be the latest one held with any of the tribes of the Iroquois in which the attempt was made to induce the Indians to espouse the cause, or to remain on terms of peace with the Americans except the successful effort in the Councils of the Oneidas. The fearful contest came; the Indians carried their own cruel, relentless mode of warfare to the fire-side, and to the homes of all the settlers along the border; and, in turn, the proud warriors of the Six Nations were driven from the soil which had once been their own, only retaining as their inheritance small and remote districts where the ancient wildwoods still overshadowed the waters of some murmuring stream - and soon the name or existence of these Indian reservations within our state became scarcely known. In these retired locations, where the Indian yet gathers around the fires kindled in the shade of their native forests, the writer of this sketch has sojourned for many days while upon a single excursion, and there listened to the story of their own eventful history as related by these children of the wilderness. The intrepid General Herkimer, who held this conference with Thayendanegea (Brant) at Unadilla, was soon called to another part of this interesting field of border-strife; and here in the lapse of only a few days, he closed his brilliant not less than glorious military career, after saving by his bravery and skill his own army from destruction, and wresting victory from the arms of imminent defeat, thus gathering the halo of surpassing and immortal glory around the latest scenes of an eventful and patriotic life, he tranquilly obeyed the summons which called him to fulfill the loftier duties of another world. In the last days of July 1777, at the time Burgoyne was making an invasion, with his large and well-appointed army, into our country from the north, St. Léger in command of a force of regulars, and accompanied by a park of artillery, together with bands of the Iroquois under the leadership of Brant, including some 1,700 men in all, also left Oswego, and with this formidable array was rapidly marching from the west to invade the Mohawk Valley.

The allied British and Indian forces arrived at Fort Stanwix, (or Schuyler) on August 3, and invested this fortress, then in a ruinous condition, and defended only by 700 troops, poorly supplied with ammunition, and commanded by the brave and skillful veteran officer Colonel Gansevoort, who had heroically determined, with the fullest concurrence of his men, to defend the fort at all hazards, and to the last extremity General Herkimer, upon approach of this hostile army which threatened to desolate that entire region with tire and with sword, at once issued a patriotic proclamation summoning the militia of the country to arms, and three regiments of the hardy yeomanry nobly responding to this call, promptly rallied around General Herkimer. The siege of Fort Stanwix had only progressed some three days, when General Herkimer commenced his march to relieve the brave defenders of this important position; and he had reached the Oriskany Valley on the morning of August 6, and after crossing the creek, the path led through low grounds, bordered on either side by a dense and heavy forest, and the vanguard of our army had scarcely began to ascent the elevated plateau beyond this pass, entirely unsuspicious of danger, when a terrific fire was rolled upon the advancing columns from every side, where amid the heavy growth of trees and shrubbery the Indians and Tories lay in ambush; and then giving the terrible war-whoop the Iroquois rushed with uplifted tomahawks upon the ranks of our army, which for a time were broken and paralyzed with dismay, while our men were falling around. General Herkimer was severely wounded, and fell from his horse, in the early part of the action, but he had the saddle taken from the horse and placed in the midst of the battlefield, and supporting himself in it then issued his orders with calmness, firmness and skill, and his men soon rallied to the fearful encounter, springing like tigers to the deadly contest - the patriots fighting hand to hand with the savages and Tories, frequently both falling together, grappling in fatal embrace, with the knifes of each sheathed in the other's bosom, while Brant ranged like some evil demon over that field, encouraging his followers in the desperate struggle. In this manner the battle continued some forty-five minutes in the meanwhile General Herkimer evinced a composure which remained undisturbed in the thickest of the fight, as in instance, he took his tobacco-box from his pocket, and striking a tinder lit his pipe, and calmly continued to smoke, while he directed the movements of our men, at the same time the bullets and tomahawks of the enemy were flying around and near him in every direction.

    As soon as the skillful orders of the intrepid Herkimer could be fully carried into effect, the American army began to regain the ground lost in the first surprise, our soldiers commenced forming and fighting in small circles. The savages had been accustomed upon seeing a soldier discharge his gun to then rush forward and tomahawk him, but this Indian artifice was turned to our own advantage on the field, by having two of our patriot-soldiers placed behind a tree, and when one had fired, the approaching savage was killed by the bullet sent with unerring aim of the other patriot. The allied British and Indians, under lead of Butler and Brant, were fast losing this fiercely contested field, and in turn wavered before the incessant fire, and the during movements of the American militia, who, encouraged and reassured by the unequaled firmness and heroism of General Herkimer, now fought with the determined bravery of veterans, and resulting from the able and effective strategic movements directed by the American general, and the promptitude and courage with which these skillful orders were executed by our troops, the ranks of the enemy, now driven from cover, were giving away, when another detachment of Tories arrived to re-enforce the British party, and the deadly struggle was again commenced with increased vigor. The opposing combatants sprang at each other with rage and relentless fury, and the entire battle field appeared like some scene in the fabled realm of Hades; bayonets were crossed in the simultaneous charge of the contending parties, they met and fought with bayonet thrust, and with clubbed-musket striking down their antagonist in the death encounter, whilst the spear, the tomahawk and the scalping-knife all were used whenever they could drink the blood of our patriot soldiers throughout all that battlefield. A diversion was now made which brought this desperate, doubtful contest at once to a favorable termination - achieving success much sooner than it could otherwise have been accomplished. General Herkimer had sent a scout to the American garrison at Fort Stanwix with intelligence of his critical position, reverberations of musketry during the battle had too been heard at the fort, and Colonel Willet, a gallant and efficient officer, immediately volunteered, accompanied by 250 men, to make a sortie to relieve the brave army which had thus encountered the common enemy while marching to the aid of the garrison who had continued to defend the fort with unyielding fortitude. Colonel Willet reaching the field of contest made an impetuous attack upon the Iroquois. The enemy, now assailed by the united American force, were compelled to yield the ground, and Brant gave the despairing signal to retreat, "Oonah! "Oonah!" Thus terminated the most severely contested battle, the most desperate and bloody contest in proportion to the numbers engaged in the combat, of any that occurred throughout the Revolution. The struggle continued for the space of six hours; the Iroquois left a hundred fallen warriors, including in the number several chiefs of the Senecas, upon the field of battle; the Americans remained the full and undisturbed masters of the field. Governor Morris, Esq., in an able address delivered before the New York Historical Society remarked instances of individual heroism that had been shown during the progress of the battle which would have added a halo to the proudest pages of the Iliad. I may add, that incidents occurred in this combat - as the unparalleled heroism of the commanding general - which would have reflected honor upon the most glorious period in Grecian or in Roman history. Never had an army been led into an ambuscade more dangerous or complete - never had a surprise thrown an army into greater dismay and confusion, and it was only through the intrepid firmness, the bravery, and the strategic ability that General Herkimer, although 80 painfully wounded, brought to the contest in this fearful emergency, that instead of meeting with defeat, our arms here achieved a real and substantial victory. We cannot indeed, properly estimate the importance which this triumph sustained in deciding the great conflict of the Revolution, or how much it had contributed to our final success. It will be remembered, that General Burgoyne was then marching with a large army through our land, and which was designed to co-operate with the allied British and Indian force that had been sent to sweep with unsparing power the

Mohawk Valley, and the repulse and discomporture which they so unexpectedly sustained in the battle of Oriskany, together with the failure to overthrow or compel the capitulation of Fort Stanwix, were the first reverses that the invading British armies had encountered. The bravery and endurance that the patriot American soldiery displayed at Oriskany and at Fort Stanwix everywhere aroused their countrymen from despondency, and inspired them with the noblest emulation; the substantial victories acquired at Oriskany and Fort Stanwix were the first that greeted the American cause in resisting the powerful and alarming invasion of 1777, and became the message to the brilliant series of triumphs which culminated in the effulgent glory that ere long had gathered around the immortal field of Saratoga. The siege of Fort Stanwix was abandoned of August 22. I have dwelt at some length on the history of General Herkimer's march, in command of the regiments of Tryon County Militia, for the purpose of relieving Fort Schuyler, and in regard to the battle of Oriskany, because these movements were made for the defense of the region bordering along the Susquehanna, and the men composing the patriot army engaged in the battle were principally residents of the region, now embraced in Delaware, Ulster and Otsego Counties, whose annals it has been my purpose to trace - and all this region, in the number of killed and wounded officers and men which were sacrificed to the cause of liberty in these memorable combats, being largely represented.

General Herkimer - after he had thus met and defeated Brant, with his allies, at Oriskany, and remained undisputed master of the battlefield - was borne upon a litter to his own residence, (a large brick mansion, erected in 1764, and situated near the present village of Little Falls, New York;) but the wound received in the action upon the 6th, did not give indication of recovery, and nine days subsequent to the battle an imputation of the wounded limb was performed, but the surgical operation had been so unskillful that it caused a profuse flow of blood, and which the surgeons did not succeed in fully stanching. General Herkimer now became aware that the hour which should be to him "the last on earth" had come, but he continued to repose upon his bed, calm and cheerful, and conversing with his friends and family in his usual pleasant manner, and with serene composure; and then calling for the Bible, the inspired and sacred word of God, the dying hero and patriot read a chapter in that blessed and only truly infallible volume ever given to mankind for their instruction and happiness and then, looking with penitence to the Savior for the forgiveness and remission of his sins, this Christian hero calmly fell asleep in the arms of death - to awake, as we will trust, amid that blessed number, the redeemed of earth, who shall enter upon that higher Life, where the spirit will forever continue to expand in the communion it will then hold with the all-pervading and supreme Beauty of the Better Land. In his life, and in the triumph of his death, we are afforded another eminent example of the power of the Christian religion to impress and to inspire the heart of men with the principles of goodness and moral truth, to awaken its devotion and entire consecration to holiness, and to give triumphant composure in the hour of the soul's departure from earth; adding another to the list of truly great men who have humbly searched the Gospel of Jesus, and who devoutly relying, with sincere faith, upon Divine Grace, have found sustenance and strength to accept the pure and holy precepts of the Scriptures as the only guide of life, and have too found hope and consolation in the promises of our Divine Savior; and as the illusions of the world were fading away, have calmly looked beyond the grave in blissful anticipation of that glorious immortality which the humble believer, the pure in heart, will there receive through the all-atoning merit of Divine Redemption.

General Herkimer had died on the evening of August 16, 1777, at the age of about sixty-five years. His remains were interred in the family burial ground, which occupies a knoll a few rods distant front the mansion. The Continental Congress, soon after decease of General Herkimer, had passed a resolution expressing in terms of grateful admiration their appreciation of his eminent services to our country, and authorizing a monument to be erected over his grave; but this resolution has never been carried into effect. Until 1847, the stranger might have searched in vain for the resting place of this patriotic and gallant soldier - the heroic and lamented martyr to the cause of American Independence. A plain marble stone, simply inscribed with, the name of the brave soldier, has since been erected over the consecrated spot where his grave had been made: although the place where the remains of this noble and eminent man repose has been permitted to pass into neglect, secluded and almost unknown. The Legislature of the State of New York would only discharge a debt which has long been justly due to the illustrious services of General Herkimer - who had laid down his life in defense of the State by rearing above his grave an enduring obelisk, and thus in marble and in bronze, perpetuate to the latest times the record of his patriotism, of his heroism, and of his greatness – *extinctus ambitur idem;* and if our State again should be invaded by a foreign foe, or be assailed by treason, and disaster and peril come, then would the sculptured form of the illustrious patriot and hero descend from the pedestal where it had been placed by a grateful posterity, to rally and to lead in the paths of victory!

The remains of an ancient Indian fortification had once existed in the town of Unadilla, within the low grounds near the Unadilla river; but, for a number of years, all traces of this extensive earthwork have been obliterated, every vestige of it disappearing from view.

A settlement had been made on the Susquehanna River, in the present town of Milford, New York, that was formed from Unadilla in 1796, by a Mr. Carr about 1770, but in consequence of Indian hostilities that was unceasingly waged against the frontier settlers during the Revolution, any material effort to maintain or make permanent addition to this early settlement was abandoned until after the close of the war. In 1783, Mr. Cully and Mr. Mulford settled within this town, and in the succeeding year a Mr. Ford, and two families by the name of Beals, all from Massachusetts, also came and made settlement near the present village of Milford.

In a conference held by sachems of the Onondaga and Cayuga Indians with the Magistrate of Albany, in 1683, the Chiefs gave a description of the Susquehanna River, and stated that Commissioners of Governor Penn had proposed to make purchase of that country - but, the Sachems mentioned that they had previously given this territory to Corlaer, (the Governor General) and they now wished to confirm the grant to Corlaer, or his representatives. This paper making the grant, and signed by the Sachems of the Cayugas and Onondagas, bears date Sepember 21, 1683. In a conference held between Sir W. Johnson and the sachems of the Six Nations and the Delaware, at Johnson Hall, and which continued from April 29 to May 22, 1765. Sir W. Johnson attempted to secure farther or more definite cessions of lands on the Susquehanna, but was in a great measure unsuccessful. The object of Sir W. Johnson, in securing a favorable boundary between the English and Indians, however, was fully attained in the Treaty held with the six nations, etc., at Fort Stanwix in 1768, and which has been previously referred to in this sketch.

A settlement had been formed near the headwaters of the eastern branch of the Susquehanna at an early period. In 1738, a patent had been granted by the Lieutenant Governor of New York, with consent of the Council, to John Lindesay, T. Roseboom, L. Gansevoort, and S. Van Shaick, for a tract of 8,000 acres of land mostly situated in a wild, picturesque valley, which was afterward named, on account of the wild cherry trees which were growing there in great luxuriance - Cherry Valley. This rural valley, in its entire extent, is about a mile in width and sixteen miles in length; the creek which rises in the upper portion of the valley, and flows along its delightful meanderings, forms the headwaters of the majestic Susquehanna; while upon the opposite side of the ridge, or elevated lands bordering this valley upon the north and the east, the tributary streams of the Mohawk take their rise. From this elevated ridge of land, whose outline here and there is gracefully broken by romantic glen and rural glade, a lovely and beautiful view stretches away before our delighted gaze nearly a hundred miles in extent, embracing the wide expanse of the Mohawk Valley, while far to the northeast are seen the dim and hazy outlines of the Green Mountains, as their loftiest elevations seem to blend with the distant horizon; while the highlands bordering this valley upon the east constitutes the first range in the wild, and romantic chain of the Catskill Mountains, which in their unequaled grandeur and sublimity, extend from this point many miles in a southeast direction, until the shadows reflected from these majestic ranges give a more gorgeous beauty to the twilight which enwraps with its loveliness the waters of the imperial Hudson; and only a few miles distant, just beyond the hills which guard the entrance of the valley upon the west, slumber the beautiful Schuyler and Otsego Lakes - fairy sheets of water, which with their wild surrounding scenery, seem indeed as if they had been brought from Eden land, and placed here, by some God of olden myth. In the early part of the succeeding year, 1739, Mr. Lindesay, having obtained full title to this tract of land from the other patentees, procured its survey into lots, and in the course of the summer removed with his family from New York, and settled amid the wild woods of the new and romantic country which he had selected for his future home. Mr. Lindesay originally came from Scotland, and was a gentleman of some distinction and fortune.

While in New York he had met with the Reverend Samuel Dunlap, and induced that gentleman to visit his patent, and being much pleased with it, he came to the conclusion also to make his residence here. In 1741, David Ramsey, William Campbell, and a number other persons, with their families, removed from Londonderry, New Hampshire, and purchased farms within the new settlement at Cherry Valley, thus adding materially to its structures of this distinguished military officer, prosperity. A schoolhouse - a rude log building, and which was also designed to answer the purposes of a church - was erected in some three or four years from the first formation of the settlement; and here, the little congregation of which Mr. Dunlap was the pastor, met in the primitive manner incident to those times, and with contrite and humble hearts seeking for that divine grace which alone could sustain them amidst the trials of earth. Mr. Dunlap also instituted a classical school at this place - the earliest one established in the province west of Albany - and students came from various and distant points to acquire from their worthy instructor the elements of the education of life.

The population of this region, how included in Otsego County, increased but very slowly prior to the Revolution. At the time of its first settlement it was embraced in Albany County; in 1772, at the time William Tryon was governor of the province, it was detached from Albany County, and formed into a new county to which was given the name of Tryon; in 1789, this name was changed to Montgomery County; and in February 1791, Otsego County, then including the two towns of Cherry Valley and Otsego, was formed from Montgomery. Before the commencement of the Revolutionary War, a few families had located in Unadilla, in Springfield, in Middlefield, in Laurens, and in Otego. The entire population of Cherry Valley was about three hundred at the beginning of the War. The exposed and critical situation of the inhabitants of these frontier settlements will thus be clearly perceived; nevertheless, they cordially united their efforts with those of the patriots' in other portions of our country in opposition to the arbitrary measures of the British ministry. The visit of Brant at Unadilla, which has been previously mentioned, caused much uneasiness in the minds of the inhabitants of this entire section of country. It was considered necessary that some fortification should be erected for purpose of defense. The residence of Colonel Samuel Campbell, at Cherry Valley, was chosen as the most favorable locality for this fortification; the house was stockaded, two block-houses were erected to give strength to the defense, and a rude redoubt embankment was constructed around the several buildings - the entire fort possessing the appointments, which if sustained by a vigilant defense, would present a formidable barrier to successful attack. In the ensuing year, when the Marquis De LaFayette was in Tryon County, he examined the strategic location of Cherry Valley, as represented upon the map; and giving due consideration to the importance of maintaining military ports for the more efficient defense of the frontiers. General LaFayette directed that a Fort should be at once erected at Cherry Valley; and, in accordance with the instruction of this distinguished military officer, a fort was constructed at this place during the early part of 1778, and the patriotic inhabitants of the surrounding country repaired to it for protection and defense. Toward the close of May 1778, Brant had came to the vicinity of Cherry Valley, with the object of acquiring information relative to the strength of the garrison defending this fort, but, being unsuccessful in these efforts through the course of the day, toward evening he stationed his party of Indian warriors near the main road, at a distance of some two miles north of the village, and here secreted himself behind a rock of some four feet in height.

On the same day, Lieutenant Wormwood arrived at the fort at Cherry Valley, with dispatches from the American forts on the Mohawk, and as evening approached, he started upon his return to the Mohawk, accompanied by an American soldier from the Fort, but they had scarcely disappeared from the gaze with which the eyes of the garrison followed the forms of their fellow soldiers into the deepening twilight, before the reverberating report of musketry came bade upon the soft evening air, and within a few minutes the horse of Lieutenant Wormwood returned, the saddle that the rider-less steed brought back, covered with tearful stains of blood. A party was at once sent out from the Fort to institute some search relative to the fate of Lieutenant Wormwood, but nothing could be ascertained to either confirm or disapprove the painful apprehensions of the garrison respecting that gallant officer during the evening. On the succeeding morning the search was renewed, and the body of Lieutenant Wormwood was then found, mutilated by the Indian s tomahawk and knife, and with its life-pulses stilled and cold in death, lying behind this large rock near the wayside. It subsequently appeared that Lieutenant Wormwood and his comrade, arriving within a short distance of this rock, under cover of which Brant and a band of his warriors were secreted, the American officer was hailed by the Indians and ordered to stop, but disregarding the summons, Lieutenant Wormwood and his fellow soldier received a volley of musketry from Brant and his followers, and Lieutenant Wormwood falling from his horse, was immediately tomahawked by Brant, and his lifeless body was dragged and hid behind this rock. The comrade of the fallen officer was taken prisoner, but giving an exaggerated account of the strength of the garrison stationed at Cherry Valley, Brant was deceived thereby, and returned to his position at Unadilla without attempting at this time to perpetrate farther mischief near Cherry Valley. In June of the same year, Brant came with a party of his warriors, and attacked and burned the adjacent village of Springfield, and upon his return from this raid carrying away a number of prisoners. Soon after the hostile incursion, it was currently reported that Brant was assembling large numbers of his warriors at Unadilla, and was fortifying that position; and, with view to ascertain the correctness of this rumor, Captain McKean, accompanied by five other patriots from Cherry Valley, made a tour along the Susquehanna. While upon this excursion he wrote a challenge to Brant, and placed it in the war path, where it would be found by the educated, though savage Mohawk Chieftain Captain McKean returned from his expedition, having taken two prisoners, and made a perilous escape from a large pursuing force of savages. Colonel Alden, in command of a continental Regiment, now assumed the defense of the Fort at Cherry Valley. In July, the tearful massacre at Wyoming was perpetrated, and upon the return of that terrible expedition, Brant resumed his position upon the Susquehanna, where he remained until autumn.

In the early days of November 1778, an expedition consisting of two hundred British Rangers commanded by Walter Butler, with five hundred Indians under command of Brant, encamped in the neighborhood of Cherry Valley - about a mile from the fort; early on November 17, while the atmosphere was hazy with the fall of misty rain, the allied

British and Indians moved from their encampment to attack the Fort, &c., at Cherry Valley, and having learned that the officers commanding the American force lodged during the night at private houses in the village, the enemy arranged that various parties should simultaneously surround the several residences of families that entertained officers of the garrison, whilst the main force would make an assault upon the Fort. The Senecas led the van. The colonel in command of the fortress, Alden, lodged at the house of Mr. Robert Welles, and although informed of the approach of the Indians seemed to be incredulous that an attack would he made upon the place. Colonel Alden, however, had only sufficient time to escape from the house before it was surrounded by the Indians, but while fleeing toward the Fort he was pursued by one of the savages, tomahawked and scalped, thus falling the first victim upon this terrible day. The Indians and Tories then entered the house of Mr. Welles, and killed him while he was upon his bended knees engaged in prayer. The Savages and Tories also killed Mr. Welles' mother, and his wife, and four of his children, together with his brother John Welles, and a sister. Miss Jane Welles, who, wherever she was known, was esteemed for her virtues and accomplishments. All belonging to the family of Mr. Welles were massacred, except one son, who was then at Schenectady attending school, who has since been widely known and distinguished as a lawyer, the John Welles, Esq. of New York. Another party of savages surrounded the residence of Reverend Samuel Dunlap, and entering it, massacred his wife; the Indians retained him, together with his daughter, as prisoners - and they treated this venerable clergyman with such cruelty that he died from its effects some months afterwards.

  Mrs. Mitchell and four of her children were murdered; one of these, a girl some ten years of age had almost recovered from the effects of the stunning blow that she had received, when another party entered the house, and a noted Tory, Newbury, with most inhuman barbarity buried his hatchet in this child's head. The Tory who perpetrated this deed of cruelty, Newbury, was arrested in the course of the ensuing season, by orders of General James Clinton, was tried as a spy, and was executed. Another band of these savage allies surrounded the house of Colonel Samuel Campbell, at the time he was absent from home and, Mrs. Campbell, together with four children, were taken prisoners, and carried by the Indians into long and painful captivity. Thirty-two of the inhabitants of Cherry Valley, and who mostly were women and children, were fiendishly massacred by the Indians, and their more savage allies, the Tories, and sixteen soldiers belonging to the garrison were also killed; and all the buildings within the village were burned, as the flames rose in lurid brightness upon the hazy atmosphere presenting a scene of magnificent, weird, and tragic grandeur. In the escape made by some families from these allied assailants, episodes of such strange and fearful character were enacted, incidents of such thrilling nature occurred, that the entire history becomes invested with a mysterious and dramatic interest. In illustration of this, I will refer to the narrative of the Clyde family. Upon the approach of the Indians and Tories on the 11th inst., Mrs. Clyde (the wife of Colonel Clyde) fled, with her children, to the forest. During the day in which the Indians were engaged in their terrible work of massacre, and throughout the long hours of storm and darkness m the succeeding night, this woman, with an infant clasped to her throbbing bosom, and with her other little ones nestling by her side, she lay sheltered behind a fallen tree of the forest; the savages, during these gloomy hours of pain and suspense, frequently passed quite near her, and once so closely that an Indian trailed his gun across the log beneath which she was then secreted. At the intercession of her husband, who had been aware of her flight to the woods, a party of American soldiers were sent out from the fort on the morning November 12, to search for Mrs. Clyde and family, and bring them, if they should be found, to the fort. In the hurried flight of Mrs. Clyde and her children on the morning of the 11th, a daughter about ten years of age became separated from the rest of the family, and had passed the night alone in the woods. When the mother was returning, with her other children, on the 12th, under escort of the party of Americans from the fort, she saw this daughter which had become separated from her on the day previous in a field near by. The child, when she saw the soldiers belonging to the party, and who were wearing blankets around their shoulders, supposed them to be Indians, and she again fled to the forest, but was rapidly pursued by several soldiers of the party, and was overtaken and brought back, and restored to the joyous embrace of her mother and the loved ones of the family. The Indians captured, and retained as prisoners at the time, between thirty and forty of the inhabitants of Cherry Valley, an uncertain fate awaited these captives - through the night, which was stormy and dark, after the savages commenced their return, these prisoners, many of whom were almost entirely destitute of apparel, were gathered around the fires which the Indians had kindled in the midst of the wildwoods where their camp was made, as the brilliant light of the flames were blended in fairy-like, fantastic way with the mysterious, gloomy shadows of the forest, while the bands of rude Indian warriors were formed into more distant groups - the whole presenting a scene of romantic, weird interest, whose gloomy, but artistic associations can not be called into existence by any effort of the imagination, but only recalled by him whose memory is conversant with similar encampments of the Indian within our wildwoods. The prisoners did not, could not, sleep through that gloomy night.

On the morning of the second day after their capture, an Indian council was held, and it was then determined to send back the larger portion of the women and children who had been taken prisoners. The Indians kept, however, Mrs. Campbell, and Mrs. Moore, together with their children, as captives; and they at once passed down the Susquehanna, then along the Tioga River, thence across to the head of Seneca Lake, and along the east shore of this lake to Kanadasaga, (an Indian castle a few miles from the present town of Geneva.) Mrs. Campbell and her children, (the mother of Mrs. Campbell, the aged Mrs. Cameron, who was an encumbrance in traveling to the Indians, was killed by a savage with a blow of his tomahawk), were taken by the Indians into western New York, and there kept as prisoners by one of the tribes for a number of months - although the members of the family during this time were separated from each other - in the ensuing season, 1779, Mrs. Campbell was taken by her captors to Niagara, when she was restored to her children, with the exception of one son, James S. Campbell. In June 1780, Mrs. Campbell was sent to Montreal - here she found her missing son, who had been kept by the Ganienkeh, a branch of the Mohawk tribe. This boy was now seven-years-old and during his captivity among the Indians he had entirely forgotten the English language, and in the meanwhile had learned the language of the Mohawks, and in this dialect expressed his happiness in again meeting his mother from whom he had been separated since they were taken prisoners by the Indians at Cherry Valley. Negotiations for some time had been pending to affect an exchange of prisoners - the American authorities to release several prisoners of distinction upon condition that Mrs. Campbell, etc., should be given up, or returned - and, in accordance with this arrangement. Mrs. Campbell, and other prisoners, were sent to Crown Point, and in a short time arrived safely at Albany. Here Mrs. Campbell was joined by her husband, Colonel R. Campbell, after an absence of two years - and the whole family was reunited. They did not return, however to Cherry Valley, until the spring of 1784; they arrived at the once delightful, and still picturesque valley which had long been their home, only to find the ruins of their former prosperity, and the marks yet remaining of the devastation which had swept this lovely region in the autumn days of 1778. Mrs. Campbell had lived to reach the age of ninety-three years - her decease occurring in 1836. She was the last survivor among the women of the Revolution, residing in the section near the headwaters of the Susquehanna. The son, who had so long been separated from Mrs. Campbell, during the painful Indian captivity, and had been restored to her at Montreal, has since been very favorably known throughout our land as the Honorable James S. Campbell; and he has already been briefly referred to in a previous chapter of this sketch.

Colonel Campbell returned, with his family, to Cherry Valley in the spring of 1784, and toward the close of summer he constructed a log house on his farm, as a place of residence. Soon after he had moved into the log dwelling - for on his first return to the valley he had hastily put up a rude cabin in which the family lived until the more substantial log building was erected - he received information that General Washington designed, and would ere long, make a journey through Cherry Valley, &c. Colonel Campbell received the visit of the illustrious Washington, who was accompanied by Governor George Clinton, General Hand, etc., within the log house which he had recently built; and the distinguished guests of this worthy family were here entertained as well, and with far more generous and cordial feeling, than they would have been in any palace amid the courts of Europe. Governor Clinton sent for a Mr. Robert Shankland, who was a resident of the vicinity, and had been distinguished in the times of the Revolution as one of the most earnest and daring patriots along the frontier; and the bold borderer soon came, and joined in the pleasant diversions of the party. When Cherry Valley was attacked by the Indians, and destroyed, Mr. Shankland's house, which was situated in a remote part of the settlement, escaped the devastation that awaited all the buildings within the village; Mr. Shankland fled, with his family to the Mohawk galley, but returned in the ensuing year with a son, Thomas Shankland, then fourteen years of age, to his former home.

Soon after he had resumed residence in his house, the Indians made an attack upon it, but he bravely and successfully defended this temporary fortress against the assault of the savages. The Indians then brought combustible materials and placed them about the house, and then applied fire, the building was soon completely enveloped in flames - in the mean- while, his son had jumped out of a window and fled toward the woods, but was captured by the Indians who surrounded the crumbling domicile upon every side. Mr. Shankland affected a successful escape. At this time, during the visit made by General Washington, the patriotic and fearless borderer was requested to give a narrative of his exploits while engaged in these partisan conflicts - and which he accordingly done - contributing by his narrative much to the enjoyment of the party. During this visit of General Washington, a gun to which attached much interest in connection with reminiscences of the Revolutionary struggle, was exhibited to the party. This gun belonged to Mr. Joseph Mayall, a patriot residing at Laurens, New York, (now included as one of the towns of Otsego County.) Mr. Mayall had once, while returning from a hunting excursion, met with a party of three men whom he undertook at their request, to plot across the Susquehanna river, when taking advantage of his situation while thus engaged in guiding the boat over the stream, they took possession of his gun, and removed the lock from it, then informed him that he must go to Canada, as their prisoner. The patriot remonstrated, but without avail - and embracing a favorable opportunity, lie seized his gun, with which he struck and killed one of the party, then discharged his piece and wounded another of the enemy, and made his escape from the other loyalist. This gun had been kept as a memento of this conflict; it had been much shattered in the encounter– and it was now viewed by General Washington and his companions in this journey, with interest. While General Washington, and his party were staying here, Governor Clinton incidentally enquired of Mrs. Campbell in regard to the number of her children, and upon informing him how many she had, the Governor added in reply "they will make fine soldiers in time," and in answer to this remark, Mrs. Campbell said, "she hoped her country would never need their services"- when General Washington made the concluding remark, "I hope so, too. Madam, for I have seen enough of war." These incidents connected with General Washington's visit, have he deemed of trivial importance, by many persons; nevertheless, every American bosom which glows with the warmth of patriotism, and throbs with emotions of gratitude as he recalls the glorious and heroic deeds of the illustrious chief of the Revolution, will dwell with pleasure upon every reminiscence which can be gathered in regard to Washington, and especially every one connected with the visit which the immortal hero and sage, whose illustrious name will continue through all time as the most honored representative of American greatness, had made to our own region of country. And, this scene which transported so long ago within this humble log-dwelling, the words which were here spoken, and the incidents which here took place, affords us a glimpse, through the vista of long intervening years, of the actual life of the men who within a brief period afterward laid the foundation of our national government - and again reveals to us the majestic presence of Washington:

"For thought on that tine brow is living still,
Such thought, as, looking far off into time,
Casting by fear, stood up in strength sublime.
When odds in war shook vale and shore and hill -
Such strength as then possessed thee, when was laid
Our deep foundation, when the fabric shook
With the wrathful surge which high against it broke,
When at thy voice the blind, wild sea was stayed.
'Tis like thee: Such repose thy living form
Wrapped round, Thou in some chained passion, breaking forth.
At times swept o'er thee like the fierce, dread north
Yet calmer, nobler, cam'st thou from the storm."

Dana.

General Washington, and the accompanying party, then proceeded to visit the Otsego Lake.

The Campbell family - the descendants of Colonel Samuel Campbell whose personal history fills such an interesting episode in the early annals of Tryon County - still reside at Cherry Valley. From the earliest settlement of the region lying near the head waters of the Susquehanna, it may be justly remarked, the members of this worthy family, in the successive generations which come and then pass away, have always exercised a commanding public influence, and have always held in the relations alike of social and public life an enviable and distinguished position. The Honorable William W. Campbell - who is a son of Honorable James S. Campbell of Revolutionary fame - I need scarcely say is very wildly known and esteemed tor his marked integrity and varied talents, as he is indeed justly distinguished as one of the ablest men not only of the region of the Susquehanna, but also of New

York State. Mr. Campbell had acquired a well-merited reputation as a lawyer of solid talents, possessing very great forensic acquirements, not less than extensive legal knowledge. And, in the discharge of important judicial duties - in the performance of the arduous labors connected with his term as Justice of the Court of Appeals of the State of New York, Judge Campbell had evinced rare ability and integrity, and fully established his fame as one of the soundest and most eminent jurists of our State. Mr. Campbell had shown before his commencement of his brilliant and distinguished judicial career- those great talents, and that comprehensive cast of intellect, requisite for the successful pursuit of the Historical researches, in winch he continued to be engaged tor some length of time. And, as the result of these investigations. Mr. Campbell had written the very interesting and reliable work - *Annals of Tryon County*, which was published in 1831. Every page of this history gives evidence of careful research - every sentence affords proof of rare ability brought to the task of its preparation; the author has indeed woven one of the fairest garlands, and in which he has twined flowers of fadeless bloom, which has yet been contributed toward that immortal wreath whose festoons adorn, with their freshness and their beauty, the glorious temple of American history.

The elegant and pleasant residence of the Honorable William W. Campbell - that was erected upon the site of the old family mansion that had been used as a fort in the Revolution - is delightfully situated in the northern part of the village of Cherry Valley, upon the public road leading to the Mohawk Valley. I may here be allowed to express the earnest wish, that the worthy and distinguished man who has his residence here, and whose name justly gives honor to this place which has always been his home, may long survive to enjoy, in the evening of his days, the rich blessings of life whose unwearied labors have been given toward advancing the knowledge, and increasing the happiness of his fellow men. Such an able and truly eminent career, marked by its rare usefulness, which has thus been quietly pursued by Judge Campbell, is indeed worthy of the noblest ambition - worthy of the most earnest emulation.

Time will not permit, nor will space allow a full narration of the interesting and important events that occurred during the Revolution in Tryon County; nor can I retrace the tragic scenes or repeat the fearful legends connected with the fierce border strife that had swept through the Mohawk Valley, and through Schoharie, is the allied British and Indians, led by the Butlers and by Brant, made frequent incursions throughout the years of 1778-81 into this extensive legion, burning and desolating the frontier settlements, and barbarously massacring the inhabitants along all the borders. As an instance of the terrible manner in which this ruthless warfare was waged against the unyielding patriots of the Revolution: a band of the Iroquois, numbering some 303 warriors, made an attack upon Cobleskill, killed twenty-two of its inhabitants, besides taking forty-two prisoners, and then plundered and burning the settlement. While this expedition was in progress, different portions of the Six Nations, upon the same day, April 18, 1779, also made savage attacks upon the American settlements at Canajoharie, at Stone Arabia and at Schoharie - burning the houses, taking prisoners and killing such of the inhabitants as were unable to escape, within these respective hamlets. During May and June 1779, particularly, the most ruthless warfare was prosecuted against the settlements along the Susquehanna and the Delaware, and in Ulster County, culminating in the battle and massacre at Minisink upon July 20, 1779. A party of sixty warriors, and twenty-seven Tories disguised as Indians, led by the Mohawk chief, Brant, arrived in the vicinity of Minisink on the evening of July 19, 1779, and waiting until the inhabitants of this place were wrapped in slumber, the Mohawk chief then made a sudden and fierce attack upon the settlement, setting fire to and burning the dwelling houses above their sleeping inmates, murdering helpless women and children, and then ravaged the place. Soon as intelligence of this raid had reached Goshen, New York, a militia force of one hundred and forty nine men were immediately mustered in Orange County, and gave rapid pursuit to the retreating enemy, whom they overtook upon the second day. Brant succeeded in leading the Americans into a partial ambush, and from the advantageous position which the Iroquois chief had chosen, a deadly fire was rolled upon the ranks of the active borderers, from eleven o'clock in the morning until the sun had sank behind the western hills, when the ammunition of the patriots failing, they were placed almost completely within the power of their cruel adversaries. The Americans had lost a large number during the desperate conflict; seventeen men who were wounded, though they appealed for mercy, were instantly massacred; Brant, himself burying his tomahawk in the brains of the brave, but wounded Colonel Wismer; and out of the entire force, 149, which had marched from Orange County, only thirty effected their escape, and returned to tell of the death of their companions in arms. These continued and fearful atrocities were the means of awakening as I had suggested in an early chapter of this sketch that full and terrible retribution which Sullivan's expedition had visited upon the Iroquois during its march through the Chemung and Seneca Lake Valleys. The Six Nations had met with complete defeat, which in effect actually dismembered their time honored Confederacy, at the Battle of Chemung; still, the Indians cherished an implacable purpose of revenge, and parties continued to ravage the Mohawk and Schoharie country until after the termination of the war. Thus Sir John Johnson, accompanied by a force of 700 of the allied British and

Indians, in May 1780, entered the Mohawk Valley, at midnight, and with fire, the tomahawk and scalping-knife, desolated its settlements. Soon after this foray in the Mohawk Valley, Sir John Johnson, in command of several companies of regulars, marching from Oswego to the Susquehanna, and at Tioga was joined by the Senecas and other tribes of the Iroquois, who were led by Thayendenagea and Corn-Planter. The combined force, amounting to some 1,500 men, supplied with three pieces of artillery, &c., then proceeded along the eastern branches of the Susquehanna to the Schoharie, and entering this fertile region, which had first been settled about 1712. The enemy, commencing their work of rapine at nightfall, October 15, 1780, remorselessly desolated its flourishing settlements, burning various hamlets throughout the valley, massacring the inhabitants, &c.; and, upon the 18th, the marauders commenced their work of devastation along the Mohawk Valley, every dwelling upon either side of the river, as far as Fort Plain, was burned, and the patriots of this region were again subjected to the terrible ordeal of Indian massacre, to which the settlers of this lovely valley were so often doomed. I have thus given detached instances of the border warfare of Tryon County; the full history of this sanguinary struggle would require volumes. The Midas of Gold - the God who receives such universal worship - however, had proffered twenty dollars for the scalp of every friend of the American cause, whether of helpless women or of innocent children, which the savages could tear from the bleeding forms of their murdered victims and bring to the British officers, thus making these midnight massacres a profitable business; and hence, according to the system of ethics which now everywhere prevails, and which approves and sustains every enterprise that "makes it pay," these atrocities committed by the savages were entirely justifiable and commendable, and the actors should accordingly be canonized as "saints."

In all the border warfare which the Iroquois had waged against the patriots of the Revolution, in the ruthless attack that had been made upon the settlements at Unadilla, Saratoga, German Flatts, Wyoming, Cherry Valley, Schoharie, Minisink and Ulster County, in accordance with the belief of the men of the Revolution, who had witnessed and who had suffered from these scenes of blood and devastation, as well as the concurrent testimony of all the early historians of the Revolutionary war, Gordon, Ramsay, Marshall, &c., Thayendanegea (Brant) was the "head and the front" - the animating master-spirit. H. K. Schoolcraft, LL.D., who had made the most extensive and elaborate researches respecting the character and history of the Indian race, thus refers to Brant: " He possessed, in perfection all the subtlety, subterfuge, art, and, when he grasped the tomahawk in active war, all the cruelty of the forest savage." (*History of the Indian tribes of the U. S.*, Vol. VI. page 284.) It may also be mentioned, that whilst the writer of this sketch was prosecuting, under authority of the State Government, surveys in western New York during 1841, and being engaged in these labors for some days upon the Indian reservations located in that section, the opportunity was afforded of a lengthy interview and conversation with the distinguished and venerable Sachem of the Senecas, Governor Blacksnake, who hail participated when a young man, in the French and Indian wars, and also in the various incursions, particularly at Wyoming, as connected with the Indian warfare waged against our frontiers during the Revolutionary war. This eminent chief of the Iroquois, at the time of our interview, had reached the extraordinary age of one hundred and seventeen years, and he was probably the latest survivor among all who had taken part in the engagement at Wyoming, Pennsylvania, in July 1778; and although he had been engaged, together with the rest of his nation, in the expeditions conducted against the patriots at the period of the Revolution, the venerable chief conversed very freely and fully, for the space of several hours, in respect to the antiquity of the aboriginal race upon our continent, the history of the Iroquois, the this time which they had opened during the war of the Revolution; and from the account which this aged and eminent sachem gave of Brant, the early historians of the Revolution, as well as the poet Campbell in the pages of *Gertrude of Wyoming*, have but justly and truthfully described the character and the career of the accomplished but cruel chief of the Mohawks, as " the Monster Brant." Governor Blacksnake had enjoyed the most ample facilities to become conversant with the various movements and hostile excursions of the Iroquois, and to know by whom they were led, he had, at an early date, as chief of the Senecas, held a position of gr eat and controlling influence among the warriors of his nation, and had negotiated a treaty with President Washington, and had afterward held conferences in relation to the affairs of the Six Nations, and with several other presidents, as John Adams, Jackson, &c.

I had called quite early in the morning of a pleasant October day, to see this venerable chief, at his residence, within the native and yet unbroken forests, through which flowed the waters of the noble Allegany River, while toward the west our view was limited by a majestic range of mountains, which were covered with luxuriant wildwoods, now tinged with the golden hues, and the crimson-tinted magnificence of autumn. The aged chief could only recall with some effort, and quite slowly, the reminiscences connected with the former glory of the Iroquois; and as he thus related the traditions connected with the history of his nation, who, within his own time, had been the sole possessors, the monarchs, of all the broad lands west of the Hudson, but which he had lived to see acknowledge the sway of another power and another race. His mind, at intervals, seemed to be drifting out from the shores of mortal life, until it seemed almost laying hold of the beautiful existence and king of the Iroquois had evinced his spirit-land. The distinguished sachem preferred to narrate the annals and traditions of the days of the lost power and greatness of his nation, mainly in the Indian dialect: and an Indian maiden, of some fifteen summers, who had received the rudiments of education, became our interpreter. This Indian maid had taken a seat upon a rude lounge or couch near the chief, and, attired in the graceful negligence of the Indian costume, her loveliness and beauty might well rival that possessed by the fairest maid of European race and, with the exception of a more brilliant hue of the dark tresses which flowed around her neck and bosom, and of a deeper tint to that rosy glow which flushed, too, over her bosom and her fair cheek, this beautiful child of the forest could not have been distinguished from the fairest lady who within our own proud halls, wandering through the mazy labyrinth of the dance. The hours had fled by half unconsciously while the aged chief thus, related the myths of Indian lore, and the rays of the setting sun were already tingeing with soft and mellowed radiance the crimson-tinted mountain forest, ere we had rested from that long conversation, and I had turned to examine some medals that the chief had received from President Washington, and other presidents, together with various mementoes which the sachem had religiously preserved. In the mean while, the fair Indian maiden, reposing upon the rude lounge, had fallen asleep, whilst her raven hair seemed to cluster more softly round her neck and bosom, and her cheek at times was flushed with a deeper, rosier glow; and thus an hour had passed ere this child had wakened from, her dreams.

It is but a simple picture - an, unpretentious scene, a slight artistic group, which had thus been formed in the home of the chief, and which I now recall from memory's mystic realm: - the aged, venerable chief, and the fair and useful maiden reposing in slumber - the little group bathed in the light of the setting sun. But, if it were represented in the beautiful and almost breathing forms which the genius, of the sculptor wakens, to life from the cold marble, it would far better illustrate the history of our time, and of the successive eras of time which continue to roll in ceaseless, course, than any written page can do; this scene, if it were embodied in the rapt and glowing beauty which lies yet unshaped in the marble block, would most truthfully picture - the history of the human race as our generation passes away only to give place to another in a succeeding age, and would indeed present a repetition of the scenes of life as they were grouped in the earliest times, even, when the first inhabitants of earth yet lingered near the lost Gardens of Eden, in the shadow of

> "The immortal trees which overtop
> The cherubim defended battlements."
> An effort has been made" in late years to gloss over the crimes committed by Brant;
> but the Mohawk chief "Hath murdered sleep,"

nor he, nor any of his apologists, can lay the haunting spirit which through all future time shall bring against his name the execution of those deeds which shall stamp his reputation; with the blackest infamy- this accusing spirit, as if it were one which erst had inhabited the living form of some victim of the Wyoming Massacre, or elsewhere, will not now avaunt at human bidding, but will affix an indelible blot upon his fame, and like Banquo's ghost, will forever echo the words of retributive doom:

> "Sleep no more to all the house."

Whilst Butler had been the acknowledged leader of the Tories, Thayendanegea was also the well-known instigator and leader of the savages in their incursions and cruel massacres and from the hatred with which he pursued the patriots of the Revolution; he seemed a personification of Attila.

It will be admitted that the friends of American independence living in Tryon County, in order to afford any protection to themselves and families against the combined attacks of the Tories and the Indians, or to conquer in this unequal contest with their allied enemies, must be under the military command of an able and efficient officer. General Herkimer had the immediate command of the Tryon militia in the early part of the war, and preceding his decease in 1778. General Phillip Schuyler, an able and judicious officer, was assigned to the chief command of the Northern Department, which embraced Tryon county, &c., and the energetic manner in which he had organized the patriot militia, and by his prompt and skillful movements disconcerted the combinations and successfully resisted the attacks of the allied; enemy, the Americans, were, enabled to shelter many of the frontier settlements from impending ruin, and to save the beautiful region of the Hudson from entire devastation. General Schuyler was born at Albany, New York, in 1733. He held a commission as captain in the New York troops at Fort Edward, in 1755, and accompanied the expedition that was sent down Lake George, in 1758, and was near Lord Howe when that nobleman fell. In 1768, Colonel Schuyler, together with George Clinton, and Nathaniel Woodhall, of Long Island, were members of the Colonial Assembly, and most ably and fearlessly advocated the rights of the colonies. Schuyler presented a series of resolutions affirming the rights of the colonies and although they were not passed, the British majority, in the power that it had previously exercised, was effectually broken. In the Second Congress, which met in the month of May 1775, Mr. Schuyler took his place as one of the delegate from New York. Washington and Schuyler were both members of the committee to whom was assigned the duty of preparing *Rules and Regulations for the Government of the Army* and from their association as members of this committee, a mutual esteem and friendship was formed, which continued to strengthen until the close of life. On June 19, 1775, Schuyler was appointed by Congress to an active command, and was assigned the rank of third Major General in the Army. In September of the same year, acting under the instructions for the invasion of Canada, General Schuyler proceeded with Generals Montgomery and Wooster as far as the Isle-au-Noix, and upon his arrival here, in consequence of the severe illness of General Schuyler, the chief command of the expedition devolved upon General Montgomery. In December 1775, General Montgomery received instructions to disarm the Tories living within Tryon County, and he performed this labor with much better success than the arduous nature of the duties that it enjoined had promised. While General Schuyler held command of the Northern Department, during the summer of 1777, General Burgoyne invaded our country from the north, with a well appointed military force of ten thousand men, which was designed to co-operate with a large force under the command of St. Léger, which had already invaded the Mohawk Valley, together with another army, which it was expected Sir Henry Clinton would lead from the South, and thus crush the country with this single movement. General Schuyler made the most active preparations to meet the invading British array; and, in the meanwhile, he skillfully obstructed and retarded its march into the interior by impeding the navigation of streams, rendering the roads almost impassable, successfully gathering provisions and military stores, and was fast rallying the militia around the American flag, preparatory to making an attack upon the invading army, which should result in certain triumph. However, in August, Gates superseded General Schuyler, while engaged in arduous exertions that promised early and complete success, in command. This change was rendered necessary, Chief Justice Marshall remarks, as a "sacrifice to the prejudices of New England." The removal of the ablest and most skillful generals in the army, from command, had also been made in other instances during the Revolutionary War - in the War of 1812 with Great Britain - and in the late Civil War in which our country was engaged to crush the rebellion; and, in all these instances, the removal of patriotic and efficient military men by superiors, who were entirely unacquainted with the strategic requirements of war, has been instrumental in postponing the triumph of our arms. In this instance, the energy of General Schuyler had laid the foundation for the important victory at Saratoga, New York; General Schuyler was elected to Congress in 1777, and was re-elected to fill the same position for throe -successive terms. In 1787, General Schuyler was chosen as a senator from New York, and ably represented our State in the first Senate of the United States; and, in 1797, he was again deputed to the U. S. Senate. General Schuyler continued to reside at Albany, in the elegant family mansion built in 1760-61, where he hospitably entertained distinguished guests from Europe, as well as the humble and poor, equally with the eminent men of our own land. Within this mansion, the Baroness Reidesel, LaFayette, Steuben, and Rochambeau, at various times, had been courteously entertained, General Schuyler died in the autumn of 1804, closing an eventful career, in which he had been distinguished alike as a military man and as a civilian, and his decease occasioned deep sorrow and mourning throughout our land.

    I have thus sketched, incidentally, the more important events that marked the border warfare of the Revolution, and of which Tryon

County was the principal theatre, as amid its hills and along its valleys had been enacted those scenes, which form one of the darkest tragedies of all time.

In giving an outline of the history of the region bordering the head waters of the Susquehanna, beside the information which I had received from Mr. Willard Cheney, who had been one of the early residents of Otsego County, and the facts derived from the aged chief of the Senecas, who had participated in the Iroquois incursions at Wyoming, and at various places in Tryon county, I have also derived aid in consulting several valuable historical works, as *Annals of Tryon County* by William W. Campbell; *Journals of the Legislative Council of New York, 1691 to 1775*, 4to.; *Historical Collections of the Essex Institute*; *History of the Indian Tribes of the U. S.*, by H. R, Schoolcraft, 4to., 6 vols.

In wandering so far from the Chemung Valley, whilst engaged in gathering anew the legends relating to those tragic events that led to the organization of the expedition of 1779, I have given an imperfect outline of the early history of the region adjoining the head waters of the Susquehanna, and, now, in retracing our steps to the Chemung Valley, will pause for a moment in this region bordering upon the Otsego Lake, whose crystal waters also fed the tributary streams of the Susquehanna, and attempt to recall a few of the interesting reminiscences connected with the sojourn in this section of the division under command of General James Clinton, while pursuing its march toward the Tioga, where a junction was formed with the brigade under the immediate command of General Sullivan – and whence our united forces then proceeded upon the important expedition of 1779, along the Chemung and Seneca Lake valleys. And while here, I too shall endeavor to recall other reminiscences which linger around the shored of this beautiful, fairy lake but I must walk lightly here, for it is sacred and hallowed ground; it has been consecrated by the presence of genius, and from the associations which thus have been thrown around this shore; it will forever remain one of the most interesting and sacred spots upon American soil. Otsego Lake forms one of the most lovely and fairy-like sheets of water to be found within our county; the lake is some nine miles in length, and is surrounded upon either side by romantic and lofty hills, the waters of the lake are very deep, and clear and beautiful, while the entire surrounding scenery possesses a wildness and beauty that belongs alone to Nature. At the time General Clinton had launched, his flotilla upon this lake, while on his way to join the flotilla of 1779, there were only two places on the shore of the lake that had been marked by civilization. "Otsego" is an Indian name, and signifies a place of rendezvous and friendly greeting. Otsego had been the original name of the lake as designated by the Indians: a rock, known as "the Otego rock," located near the outlet of the lake, is affirmed by tradition to have been the precise spot where the red men of the forest had been accustomed to meet from an immemorial period. The present village of Cooperstown, New York is at this place. In 1737, the footsteps of civilized man had probably first pressed the shores of the beautiful lake, since known to the world by the name so long given to it by the Indians, the Otsego. One hundred and thirty years ago; Cadwalder Colden, Surveyor General of the Province of New York, it appears, visited the place where Cooperstown is now situated, making at that early date an examination of the region surrounding the lake and the Susquehanna river, to both of which Mr. Colder refers in his report. The next account in relation to the country about the Otsego Lake being visited by the white man, is contained in the journal of the Reverend Gideon Hawley, where this missionary, under date of "May 31, 1775," refers to the difficulty in obtaining a canoe, and thus incidentally makes mention of this lake: "In afternoon came from Otsego Lake," &c.

This place - the shores lying lovely village of Cooperstown now stands, is said to have also been frequented, by Indian traders for a long time preceding the earliest permanent settlement made in the vicinity. A patent for a tract of land lying near the Otsego Lake, had been granted to John C. Hartwick, in an instrument bearing date April 22, 1701, and, about the year 1765, Mr. Hartwick commenced to make a clearing near the outlet of the lake, but subsequently becoming convinced that these improvements had been made outside the limits of his estate he soon relinquished it altogether and abandoned the place. Thus terminated the first attempt, so unsuccessful in its results, to form a settlement near Otsego Lake. In 1768, as previously mentioned in this sketch, Colonel George Crogan had secured a conveyance of a tract of land from the Indians, amounting to one hundred thousand acres, lying upon the west side of the lake, and of the Susquehanna River; and in 1769, a patent was given by the Colonial Government of New York, securing this same parcel of land to Colonel Crogan, and others. It appears that Colonel Crogan bad obtained a loan of three thousand pounds sterling, through the agency of Governor William Franklin, of New Jersey, and had given security for payment of this sum. On December 2, 1709, the other persons to whom the patent had been granted, beside Colonel Crogan, conveyed to him in three separate instruments, the full title and legal rights to this tract of land; the original patent, and three conveyances, are undoubtedly the earliest legal instruments making conveyance of real estate with the term of Otse. On March 10, 1770. Colonel Crogan gave, as additional security for payment of the three thousand pounds before mentioned, a mortgage on that portion of this tract of land, since known as "Cooper's Patent"; and in March 1773, a judgment was obtained in the Supreme Court of the colony of New York against Colonel Crogan, upon the bond which had accompanied the mortgage. And, finally, all the securities resting upon this patent, as early as the month of May 1785, where assigned to William Cooper and Andrew Craig, of Burlington, New Jersey. In autumn 1785, Mr. Cooper, accompanied by several surveyors, made a visit to the land that he had thus secured in the vicinity of Otsego Lake, arriving here by the route of Cherry Valley and Middlefield; and, in January of the succeeding year, 1786, Mr. Cooper commenced a settlement upon his land - choosing a pleasant and delightful location near the shores of the beautiful Otsego Lake. Previous to the settlement thus made in the winter of 1786, by Mr. Cooper upon the site of the present village of Cooperstown. Mr. Hartwick had made an attempt to form a settlement here, as before stated; and Colonel Crogan, with his family, had also made their home at this place for a brief period, and while here had erected, it is believed, a mock-house, some fifteen feet square, constructed of hewn logs, and which was the first building, it is supposed, erected in the region adjacent to the Otsego Lake. This building remained standing until 1797 or 1708, when it was taken down, and the logs of which it was constructed were removed by Mr. H. P, Eaton, and set up near his residence as an out-house.

It should he mentioned, however, that previous to the time the first permanent settlement had thus been commenced by Mr. Cooper near the Otsego Lake, this region had been connected with memorable events, and interesting episodes in American history, which will forever render it hallowed ground, and give it an important place in the annals of our country. Cooperstown had been the scene of stirring incidents not less than pleasant associations, connected with our early history, which will ever continue to gather around its name the most sacred reminiscences.

In spring 1779, General James Clinton, in command of a brigade designed to co-operate with the force under General Sullivan in prosecution of the campaign against the Iroquois, had ascended the Mohawk as far as Canajoharie, New York, and upon his arrival at this place General Clinton sent an expedition, consisting of some five hundred men, under command of Colonel Van Schick, accompanied by Lieutenant Colonel Willet, with rendezvous at Fort Schuyler, against the Onondagas. This expedition proceeded at once to destroy the Onondaga castle, burned fifty houses, killed some thirty warriors, and took thirty-seven prisoner, thus completely accomplishing the purposes of the expedition, and returned in six days from the commencement of the march, to the main army under command of Clinton. General Clinton, then commenced, after the return of this expedition, to open a road through the wilderness, from Canajoharie to the head of Otsego Lake, a distance of some twenty miles. This labor was difficult and arduous; this military road was required for the passage of artillery, and for the transmission of numerous boats, and the entire labor connected with this march called forth the utmost fortitude and endurance of our brave and hardy soldiery. Traces of this military road, known as the "Continental Road," can still be seen. General Clinton had commenced his arduous march from Canajoharie on the June 17, 1779, and had opened this road through the forest, and across a hilly region of country, and succeeded in reaching the head of Otsego Lake, or Springfield, on June 30, 1779. General Clinton then proceeded with his division, who were embarked in boats on the lake on July 1, 1779, to the foot of Otsego Lake, and encamped his troops upon the site of the present village of Cooperstown. General Clinton here established his quarters, in the block- house referred to which had been erected before the expedition of 1779, and which was situated in the grounds. The troops under command of General Clinton, remained encamped near the Otsego Lake for the spare of several weeks, or from about the first of July to the first week in August. Whilst the troops were encamped at this place, they were exercised every day in efficient military drill. Two spies, who had been captured while the army was pursuing its march from the Mohawk Valley to the region of Otsego, were tried by courts martial during the time the troops were thus encamped near the outlet of the lake, and were sentenced to be shot. General Clinton reprieved the sentence of one of these deserters, who was named Snyder - the sentence of the other was promptly carried into effect, the deserters being executed at a spot lying upon the west side of the lake, near the outlet. Two spies had previously been executed while the army was encamped at Springfield, during the progress of its march from the Mohawk Valley to the Otsego Lake. One of these, Hare, was a lieutenant in the British service - the other Newberry, was the infamous spy who has before been referred to in connection with his ruthless hatchery of the infant child of the Mitchells, at Cherry Valley. Whilst the troops commenced by General Clinton were encamped at the foot of the Otsego Lake, aside from the daily drill they were not idle. Owing to the drought of the summer season, the waters at the outlet, that afforded communication from the lake to the Susquehanna, had become very low, and they were also somewhat obstructed by flood-wood, and thus from both causes, setting a barrier to their navigation; and accordingly the troops were employed in the construction of a dam across the outlet of the lake, which raised the waters in the lake to a sufficient height, that, upon removal of this artificial dam, the accumulated floods not only removed the obstruction of flood-wood. &c., but also safely carried the numerous flotilla, numbering two hundred and fifty boats, and upon which were embarked the troops, cannon and stores connected with the army, down the channel to the Susquehanna - the force under command of General Clinton forming a junction at Tioga with the main army, commanded by General Sullivan, upon August 22, 1779. Some traces of this dam, thus constructed by General Clinton's troops, remained visible until a very recent period, near Cooperstown. A large iron swivel, which was said to have been buried by Clinton's troops, while they were encamped at this place, was found in digging the cellar of the house first; occupied by Judge Cooper. This piece of artillery, named the "Cricket," was the only one, for a number of years, that was used for the purpose of salutes, rejoicings, &c, by the citizens of Cooperstown; and finally it burst while being used in celebrating the anniversary of our national independence.

Mr. William Cooper, as previously remarked had come to the vicinity of Otsego Lake in the autumn of 1785, accompanied by a party of surveyors. It should be mentioned that in 1783, while General Washington was making a tour of observation throughout a portion of our country, then so recently formed into an independent empire, after he had made the visit at the Chemung Valley, before referred to in this sketch, the illustrious hero and statesman then proceeded to visit the beautiful Otsego Lake, passing along the lovely region where the village of Cooperstown is now situated; thus, the immortal Washington was the first actual explorer, after the conclusion of peace, of the region of the Otsego Lake, and he was the first to perceive the great natural advantages which it possessed - and his foot-steps, which once were pressed upon this soil, have made it hallowed ground.

General Washington thus describes this tour, and alludes to his visit to the Otsego Lake and the headquarters of the Susquehanna, in a letter addressed to the Marquis de Chastelleaux, all extract from which I will here give:

"Princeton, October, 12, 1783.

My dear Chevalier - I have not had the honor of a letter from you since the 4th of March last. I have lately made a tour of the lakes George and Champlain as far as Crown Point- then returning to Schenectady, I proceeded up the Mohawk River to Fort Schuyler (formerly Fort Stanwix) crossed over Wood Creek that empties into the Oneida Lake, and affords a water communication with lake Ontario. I then traversed the country to the head of the eastern branch of the Susquehanna, and viewed the lake Otsego, and the portage between (that lake and the Mohawk River at Canajoharie. Prompted by these actual observations, I could not help taking a more contemplative and extensive view of the vast inland navigation of these United States.

I am, dear Chevalier,
Your most obedient,

George Washington."

Thus this great and illustrious man - "First in war, first in peace, and first in the hearts of his countrymen" - was the first to visit, solely for the purpose of a visit the region of the Otsego Lake. As his eye then drank in the matchless beauties of its wild, romantic scenery, this visit, made at such an early date, forever afterward consecrated the shores of the lovely Otsego, giving it a sacred place among

The Delphian vales, the Palestines,
The Meccas of the mind,"

The first permanent settlement that was made upon the site of the present village of Cooperstown had been formed in 1786; during this year several persons came and located here. A widow lady, by the name of Johnson, with her family, were undoubtedly the earliest permanent residents in Cooperstown. They, at first, lived in a log house, but in the spring of 1786, Mrs. Johnson had a frame house erected, which she sold, during the course of the summer to Mr. William Ellison, the surveyor, who removed the house, the same season, to a place near the outlet, and now included in the grounds of Edgewater. This house, which was the earliest frame building constructed within the present village of Cooperstown, was two stories in height and of respectable dimensions; it was applied for the purpose of a tavern. In June, 1786, Mr. John Miller, accompanied by his father, arrived in the vicinity of Cooperstown, then inhabited only by the family of Mrs. Johnson above mentioned; and Mr. Miller is still a resident of Cooperstown - the latest, and one of the most honored survivors among the early pioneers of the region of the Otsego Lake. On the arrival of Mr. Miller, with his father, at this place, they felled a large pine tree across the river, near the outlet, to answer the purpose of a bridge over the stream. The stump of this tree, upon which was inscribed, in white paint, the words "Bridge Tree," was located within the grounds of Lakelands. During 1787, a bridge, constructed of log-abutments and log-sleepers, upon which was placed a rude platform of logs, was built near the outlet. This was the first bridge that allowed the passage of wagons, constructed across the Susquehanna near Cooperstown. Mr. Israel Guild, William Abbott, and James White, also came during 1786, and settled near the outlet of the lake. It is believed, however, that no families remained near Cooperstown during the ensuing winter, excepting those of Mrs. Johnson, Mr. Guild and Mr. Ellison. Early in the succeeding year, Mr. William Cooper, accompanied by his wife, who then came upon a visit, arrived near the lake. In the same year, a number of emigrants, mostly from Connecticut, settled near the outlet, constructing log dwellings upon the site of the village of Cooperstown.

In the early part of 1788, Mr. William Cooper had commenced the erection of his dwelling house, which was the second house of any considerable size built in Cooperstown. The house was two stories in height, with two wings attached. It commanded a fine view of the lake, and, as originally built, stood immediately in front of the mansion now known as the Hall. This building had been represented upon an early map of Cooperstown, where it is designated as "Manor House." This house was removed a short distance in 1799, and in 1812 it was completely destroyed by tire. Mr. Guild continued to reside in the blockhouse, before referred to, until 1789. The house which had been occupied by Mr. Ellison was pulled down in 1812.

In 1789, Mr. Cooper completed the erection of his residence; but he did not remove his family to Cooperstown until October, 1790, at this date giving up his residence in New Jersey entirely. During the preceding winter, however, Mr. Cooper had brought a stock of merchandize into the village, and opened a store, a Mr. R. R. Smith transacting the business as merchant in this establishment. In 1790, according to an old document, Cooperstown included, among the buildings it then contained, seven frame houses, three frame barns, &c. From this date, the growth of the village steadily and rapidly progressed. Otsego County was formed February 16, 1791, and Cooperstown was designated by law as the county seat. William Cooper, upon the organization of the county, received the appointment as first judge of its courts; and Richard R. Smith was appointed sheriff. A courthouse, thirty feet square in dimensions upon the ground, and two stories in height, was built; the lower story, consisting of four rooms, was constructed of hewn logs; the second story, used for the purposes of a court room, was made of frame-work. In this year, 1791, during the summer season, the old Red Lion Tavern was built. Several other commodious buildings were also erected in the course of the season.

Abraham TenBrock, Esq., from New Jersey, who was the earliest lawyer residing at Cooperstown, came to the village in 1791. Mr. J. G. Fonda, Mr. Joseph Strong, and Mr. Moss Kent, who were respectively members of the legal profession, came and settled at Cooperstown in the course of one or two years. These gentlemen were the earliest lawyers, engaged in the duties of their profession, resident in the village. Dr. Fuller, who was the first physician of any prominence or standing in the place, arrived at Cooperstown in June 1781, and continued actively and successfully employed in the labors incident to his profession, at this place, for the long term of forty-six years. For a considerable time, a space of many years, nearly all of the medical practice in the county was entrusted to Dr. Fuller. The first school in the village of Cooperstown was taught by Mr. Joshua Dewey, and was commenced about 1792 or 1798. Mr. Dewey was born in Lebanon, Connecticut in 1767. He entered college at the age of seventeen, and removed to Otsego County in 1791; and, in the school that he established at Cooperstown, J. Fennimore Cooper received his earliest school instruction, here learning his A. B.Cs. Mr. Dewey afterward represented the county of Otsego in the State Legislature. Mr. Dewey was succeeded, as teacher of the early schools kept at Cooperstown, by Mr. Oliver Cory, who gave instruction in the elementary branches of education during five days in the course of the week, reserving every Saturday for the purpose of instructing his scholars upon moral and religious subject - the most essential department in the education of life, but which has now become so sadly neglected in the lessons taught either in our common schools or academies. Mr. Cory had first held his school in the courthouse building, and subsequently taught in the first schoolhouse, which was a small wooden building that was erected in the place. He was employed as teacher in the schools at Cooperstown for many years. He had been remembered with kindness by a large number of the prominent citizens of Cooperstown, who had once been his pupils; and he departed this life only a few years ago, deeply lamented by all who knew this estimable man. The first public library established in the village was opened March 11, 1796. Timothy Barnes was appointed, and acted as librarian in this institution.

The first child's birth in Cooperstown was in 1792. The child was Nathan Howard, a son of Mr. John Howard. Mr. W. Abbott, who belonged to the village community, but did not actually reside in the village, had a son born some time previously to the birth above mentioned as taking place, in the village. This child was christened "Reuben." Another birth had occurred upon the patent at Fly Creek, at as early as 1787. The earliest death within the village occurred October 11, 1793; the deceased was a son of Mr. Griffin, and he was buried in a piece of ground then selected for purposes of interment situated where Christ's Church now stands. The earliest post route, reaching Cooperstown was organized in 1794. This was in accordance with the Act, which passed the Legislature on the May 8, 1794, establishing a post route from Albany to Canandaigua and leading through Cherry Valley, Cooperstown, &c. The post office, which was placed under the charge of Joseph Griffin, as postmaster, was opened on June 1, 1794, at this place.

The earliest religious exercises pursued upon the Sabbath, at Cooperstown, were conducted by Reverend Mr. Morley, a Presbyterian clergyman, who remained at the village for the period of six months in the year 1793. A short time after his arrival in the place, or around August 1795, the Presbyterian church, the first religious organization in the village, was formed. The Presbyterian house of worship, a structure of wood, sixty-four feet in length by fifty in width, was afterward built, and dedicated upon August 6, 1797. In September 1797, the Reverend Thomas Ellison, Protestant Episcopal clergyman, from Albany, made a visit to Cooperstown, and while here, held service in accordance with the rites of the Episcopal church, in the courthouse. The first organization of the Episcopal church in Cooperstown, however, was made January 1, 1811, under the name of Christ Church, and the Reverend Donald Noah was chosen as rector, and he continued to hold this office, informally, down to the period of his death, which occurred in 1799. In 1793, Reverend John Frederick Ernst, a Lutheran clergyman, was employed by communicants of his religious sect, to conduct the exercises pertaining to their denomination: but he remained in the village for the period of only two years. In 1799, the Reverend John McDonald, an estimable clergyman and classical scholar, came to Cooperstown and was engaged in conflicting religious exercises, but, like his Divine Master, he was poor, and "had nowhere to lay his head." He was arrested for debt, and was placed upon the limits; but during his imprisonment, he continued to preach regularly in the courthouse, to the congregation that assembled, to listen to his beneficent teachings. It has always been, as it is now, that if a man has the moral courage, the nobleness of soul, to lead an earnest and pure life, and to be content with honest poverty, he will be sure to receive the unjust censure and the unmerited persecution of the world. Thus Carlyle, the most profound and philosophical thinker of our age, in alluding to like persecutions of worthy men, truthfully remarks: "Thus persecuted they the prophets, not in

Judea only, but in all lands where men have been," Suffering and starvation, imprisonment and crucifixion are the rewards which men always give to the true and noble benefactors of the race - the glorious martyrs, whose immortal names are inscribed in imperishable glory upon the roll of fame.

These were the earlier religious exercises and church services that had been regularly instituted at Cooperstown. Other religious denominations, as the Baptist, &c., had organized churches and erected, houses of worship, at a later date, in the village.

In 1795, the worthy enterprise of establishing an academy at Cooperstown, was rejected. The academy edifice, which was sixty-five feet in length by thirty-two feet in width, was secured upon September 18, 1795. Tuition in the English branches of instruction was given in this institution, leaving studies in the department of classical learning to be elsewhere pursued. This academy, however, acquired some distinction. In September 1797, it was visited by two of the Regents of the State University, the State Lieutenant Governor, and the Reverend Thomas Ellison. The Cooperstown Classical and Military Academy, where pupils received thorough military instruction, was in successful operation for sometime, reaching its zenith of prosperity about 1839. The students were at one time reviewed by General Sandford. The Cooperstown Seminary was instituted in 1853-54. The seminary edifice was commenced in June, and the framing completed, and building erected in August. The entire structure was finished in four months from its commencement, Mr. L. M. Bolles being the architect. The school was opened on November 15, 1854, its faculty, at that time, consisting of sixteen professors and teachers. It was dedicated on November 17, 1854, Bishop Simpson, etc., delivering address upon the occasion.

In the spring of 1795, the *Otsego Herald or Western Advertiser*, this was the second journal published in the state west of Albany, was established at Cooperstown; the first number of the paper being issued upon April 3, 1795. Mr. Elihu Phinney was the editor and proprietor of the *Otsego Herald*. It was published in folio form, and the quality of the paper upon which it was issued, was very coarse, and its color was nearly blue.

This newspaper was continued by its first proprietor until the period of his decease, in 1813, and it was then issued by his sons, H. & E. Phinney until 1821.

Eleven different newspapers, beside the *Herald*, at various periods, have been published at Cooperstown. These papers were called the *Impartial Observer*, the *Cooperstown Federalist, Freeman's Journal, The Switch, The Watch Tower, The Tocsin, The Otsego Republican*, and the *Otsego Examiner*. The publication of *The Country Magazine* was commenced at Cooperstown, in 1852, but only continued for the space of a few months.

The earliest military organization near Cooperstown was formed in 1794. A volunteer company of cavalry, Benjamin Griffin, Captain, was then established, the earliest regular organization of the militia, however, was not effected until 1798. Jacob Morris, of Butternuts, New York, being the first brigadier general, and Francis Herring, the first colonel, in the regiment that included the village, John Howard was the first captain of the militia company formed in Cooperstown. He drowned in the Susquehanna in 1799, and was succeeded by William Sprague. And independent military company of artillery, was established in 1798, of which William Abbott was Captain S. Huntington, lieutenant; G. G. Walker, second lieutenant.

On several occasions during the early history of Cooperstown officers of the federal government established recruiting parties in the village the first time in 1799, when hostilities with France were threatened. Lieutenant J. C. Cooper, then enlisted some thirty men in the company which he commanded; and the second time in 1812, when Captain Grosvenor raised, a detachment of riflemen, here.

The growth of Cooperstown between 1775 and 1805, was gradual, but continued steadily to advance. Near the close of the year 1796, Judge Cooper made his contract for the building of the hall. This was undoubtedly the most elegant private residence, at the time of its erection, west of Schenectady. The house was commenced in 1796, and was completed in June 1799, when the family of Mr. Cooper removed into their new home. This pleasant mansion still remains one of the finest structures in this section of the state, and the largest and most elegantly constructed building that has yet been constructed in the village of Cooperstown.

Richard Fennimore Cooper, Esq., selected Apple Hill as the site for his proposed residence in the village, at an early date, and in the year 1800, he had his private mansion erected upon this spot. His house was the second one constructed in the manner of a villa, built in the village. In year 1803, John M. Bowers, Esq., who was the owner of an estate bounded on its western limits by the Susquehanna and the Otsego Lake, arrived in the vicinity of Cooperstown, and commenced during the same year, the erection of his residence at Lakelands. The house was completed, and its proprietor moved into it in 1804. This place is not actually within the limits of Cooperstown, but its occupants belong to the village community. Messrs. John Russell, Elijah J. Metcalf, and Robert Campbell, all of whom were men of marked distinction and ability, came to Cooperstown between the years 1795 and 1802, and became permanent residents. Mr. Russell was the second member of Congress sent from this place. Judge

Metcalf deceased in 1821, but the other two of these gentlemen lived to pursue a long and distinguished career of public usefulness, receiving the respect and honors that continued to he so justly awarded them. In 1802, John Miller constructed a brick house, which was the second one built in the place. In 1804, Judge Cooper caused a stone building to be erected, which was designed and used as a residence for his daughter, who had married Mr. Pomeroy, who came from Massachusetts and located in Cooperstown in 1801. This house was the first stone building erected in the village. In 1810, Isaac Cooper, Esq., commenced the erection of his house at Edgewater, but this elegant residence was not completed until some three or four years afterward. In 1807, an act had passed the Legislature providing for the incorporation of the place, as "the Village of Otsego," but, as a majority of the inhabitants of village were dissatisfied with the provisions of this act, they remained a dead letter upon the statute book. A new law, incorporating the place as the village of Cooperstown, was enacted on June 12, 1812. At this time, the village contained 133 houses and numbered 686 inhabitants. The original proprietor of the village plot, William Cooper, Esq., and to whose capacity and energy the village of Cooperstown, not less than Otsego County, was principally indebted for its great and substantial growth and prosperity during the early period of the settlement of the region of the Otsego. After he had been a permanent resident of the village for nineteen years, died on December 22, 1809.

Judge Cooper had reached the age of fifty- five years at his decease, which occurred at Albany. His name, more prominently than that of any other citizen of Cooperstown, is identified with the early history of the place. Mr. Cooper had been appointed in 1791, as the first judge of Otsego County, organized in that year. He had also been elected in 1794, as Member of Congress, and was the first representative of the district in the National Legislature, where he remained, I believe, by virtue of repeated elections, during the continuous and long period of seventeen years.

The visit of Washington to the spot where Cooperstown is now located has already been mentioned. This place has also been visited at various times by other distinguished gentlemen. Talleyrand, the eminent diplomatist, during his sojourn in our country, had passed a number of days in the village of Cooperstown, making his home, whilst here, beneath the hospitable roof of Judge Cooper. An acrostic, written to Miss Anna Cooper, and which was inserted in the *Otsego Herald* of October 2, 1795, has been ascribed to the facile pen of the accomplished French diplomatist. This verse commenced as follows:

"*Amiable philosophe, au printems du son age.*"

It may be mentioned that Miss Cooper, to whom these lines were addressed, was killed in falling from a horse in the town of Butternuts, on September 18, 1800, and her funeral sermon was preached by Reverend D. Nash, and she was buried in accordance with the rites of the Protestant Episcopal Church, then, for the first time, performed in the village of Cooperstown. It is said that Talleyrand was much delighted with his visit here, in the midst of the quiet and romantic scenery of the Otsego Lake, and mingling in society which might challenge favorable comparison with the aristocracy of the proud French capital.

On September 17, 1806, Governor Lewis, the Executive of the State of New York, at the time, accompanied by Adjutant-General Van Rensselaer, made a visit to Cooperstown. In September 1839, the Honorable Martin Van Buren, then President of the United States, visited Cooperstown. The President, who had come from Fort Plain in company with Judge Nelson, and several other distinguished citizens of Cooperstown, was escorted into the village by several hundred inhabitants of the place, and the great statesman was enthusiastically received by large numbers of his political friends, residents of Otsego, who had assembled near the Eagle Hotel; the Honorable E. B. Morehouse welcoming President Van Buren to their midst by an appropriate address, and to which Mr. Van Buren made an able and eloquent reply. I may here remark that President Van Buren possessed a great, sagacious and comprehensive mind that grasped and successfully solved the most difficult and most profound questions of public policy, and his public career, in which he had discharged with eminent ability and integrity the responsible and important duties connected with the offices that he held at different times as Governor of the State of New York, Senator in the United States Congress, Secretary of States, in connection with President Jackson's administration, Vice-President of the United States, and President of the United States, has indeed given Mr. Van Buren an eminent rank with the great and illustrious statesmen of our land. The rare and fascinating social qualities which Mr. Van Buren possessed, always ready to respond to the calls made upon his attention by his fellow-citizens, have also given him an endearing claim to the grateful remembrance of his countrymen. President Van Buren remained at Cooperstown for several days, participating in a cordial and friendly interchange of views with other distinguished men of that period, who occupied the front rank among the jurists and legislators of our country - the Honorable Samuel Nelson, and Honorable John H. Prentiss - the compeers of such men as Story, Kent, Benton, Clay, and Webster. Whilst I thus gaze through the vista of the past, and recall this scene, I can again see the majestic form of Mr. Van Buren mingling in this group, which his calm, comprehensive intellect rules its discussions, and gives to its associations the lofty earnestness and grandeur that characterized that epoch in our national history:

"And years, as if by magic flee.
And leave us in his grand old time."

Among the distinguished men who thus welcomed President Van Buren to their midst at Cooperstown, and with whom that illustrious statesman then so cordially associated, I believe the Honorable Samuel Nelson is now one of the latest surviving representatives; as he is, indeed, almost the last representative of that more glorious era in the history of our country, which with our mourned and departed statesmen, has passed away forever. The Honorable Samuel Nelson was born in Washington County, New York. He pursued his studies, and graduated at Middlebury College, in Vermont, and afterwards read law. In 1817, he commenced the practice of his chosen profession in Cortland County, New York, where by the exercise of his brilliant legal abilities he soon acquired an extended and permanent forensic reputation. He received the appointment of Circuit Judge in 1823, and discharged the arduous duties attached to this position with unsurpassed and rare ability and honor for a number of years. Whilst Mr. Nelson was thus engaged in the performance of his labors as Circuit Judge, or about the year 1825, he removed to Cooperstown. Mr. Cooper here married the only daughter of Judge Russel, and made his residence for some time at Apple Hill; but in 1827, purchasing Fennimore; he enlarged the house then upon the premises, remodeling it into a commodious and elegant family mansion.

In 1833, Mr. Nelson received an appointment to another and still more elevated judicial position, being promoted to the bench of the Supreme Court of the State of New York; and, in 1831, he was appointed

Chief Justice of the State. This eminent position, in which Judge Nelson was now called to act, ruling by his superior legal ability and knowledge the deliberations of this august judicial tribunal, has indeed been adorned by the labors of several of the most learned and distinguished jurists of our land, and whose reputation will rival that earned by the most illustrious jurists of other lands; but the pure and lofty fame which Judge Nelson had here so nobly won, the ermine which he had thus worn for the period of fifteen years, whilst discharging the duties of the most exalted judicial position within the State, in its purity, and its simple, majestic grandeur, has as yet been unrivalled - yet gathering around it the highest forensic glories of out State. At the period of the history in our State when Judge Nelson received his appointment, the State Judiciary sustained a much higher position, as far as the ability, soundness and learning of its members were concerned, than it has for the past few years. The appointing power was then vested in the hands of those who brought wisdom and experience in making choice of judicial officers: but now it is lodged with the people - large numbers of who are ignorant of the policy of our laws, and even ignorant of the names of the candidates for whom they cast their suffrage. This evil - the extension of suffrage, or placing the supreme power of the state in the hands of ignorant classes, who were incapable of exercising this sovereignty in accordance with their own knowledge, but were led and controlled by other and more artful men, had been the principal cause in accomplishing the ruin and downfall of the old Republics, and this evil, in our own land, now constitutes the great danger, than which none greater can exist, to the stability and permanence of our own Republic. The Federal Judiciary has always constituted the great safeguard not only to the liberties and to civil rights of the citizens of the Republic, but also to the permanence of the Republic itself. The counsels of this body, as it is formed by the Constitution, are subject only to the control of calm and enlightened reason and law, and are swayed neither by the dictation of arbitrary authority, nor by popular clamor, but uninfluenced by the excitement of the passing hour, applies the fixed principles of the Constitution in testing the validity of all acts and enactments. In 1845, Judge Nelson received appointment as one of the Associate Justices of the Supreme Court of the United States; and he has now performed the duties of this position for a longer time and the commencement of his official labors dates further back than the services of any other member of the Supreme Court of the nation. Fortunately for the security of American liberty, and the stability of our free institutions and laws, the Supreme Court - from the time that Marshall had presided over its deliberations, down to its recent sessions - was ruled by the master-mind of the eminent Chief Justice, Chase, who is alike distinguished as a jurist and a statesman - has invariably been composed of the ablest jurists, most candid and upright men of our nation. Political prejudices and excitements, which have swayed other branches of the government, have not influenced this august judicial tribunal. It is but simply just to say, that, lofty as always has been the prestige of the Supreme Court. It has been amply sustained by the eminent legal erudition, the profound and varied forensic learning, not less than the recognition of the comprehensive principles of justice in the arbitration of cases coming under his jurisdiction, which has ever marked, in a pre-eminent degree, the career of the illustrious jurist - the Honorable Samuel Nelson. The judicial opinions, and decisions which have been given by Judge Nelson, have always been marked by the clear and logical force of their arguments, sustained by an unanswerable array of facts, and a profound exposition of the principles of constitutional law, and addressed to the reason and the judgment, and they will take their place in history as models of eloquence -majestic and beautiful, and unadorned save by their truth and exhaustless learning. In the discussion of the legal questions involved in these opinions. Judge Nelson has indeed evinced that giant grasp of mind, the massive strength of judgment, the great argumentative power, which have so fully shown the unmatched proportions of his colossal intellect, and which, added to long experience, has given to Judge Nelson the pre-eminent fame as one of the ablest and wisest, not less than the most illustrious jurist now living in our state, or in our country. Excepting the time when Judge Nelson has been absent to sessions of the Supreme Court, he has resided at Cooperstown, making his home in this pleasant village for the past forty years, well known for his many virtues, the purity and excellence of his moral character, and the unobtrusive greatness of intellect which give shape to the truly eminent character of this illustrious man. Long may the village of Cooperstown be honored by his living presence, and profit by the force of his example; and when he shall depart from earth to be admitted to the courts above, the influence of his life will continue to endure and gather strength, and his own great fame shall indeed be immortal - and then, the simple fact that his home had been in Cooperstown, will ever constitute one of the most brilliant honors in its escutcheon that history can record.

Among the other distinguished men who had welcomed President Van Buren to Cooperstown, in 1839, and had also accompanied the great New York statesman from this place to Cherry Valley, were the Honorable E. B. Morehouse, and Honorable John H. Prentice - already referred to in these papers. Judge Morehouse was born at Hillsdale, Columbia County, New York, about the year 1791. He came to Cooperstown in 1815, here studied law, and entered upon the labors connected with his profession, which he successfully pursued for many years, a portion of this time being engaged as District Attorney. At the first State election under the State constitution of 1846, he was elected as Judge of the Supreme Court of the State, and drawing for the long term, had six years to serve in this capacity, from January 1, 1850. But the angel of death came to summon him to the tribunals above. He died on Dec. 16, 1849. At a meeting of the Otsego bar, held soon after his death, resolutions expressive of the loss that the profession and the community had sustained, were passed.

The Honorable John H. Prentice was born in Worcester, Mass., April 17, 1784. On January 8, 1803, Mr. Prentice arrived at Cooperstown, and at once established the *Freeman's Journal*, of which he was the editor and publisher, with the exception of ten or twelve months, until January 1849. Mr. Prentice was representative in Congress during the four years of President Van Buren's administration, and sustained politically the policy of the President. Colonel Prentiss had taken a prominent part in assisting the worthy enterprises of Otsego County for half a century, and was regarded as a leader in public affairs here. He died, after an illness of some three months, on June 26, 1861.

In 1828, the Honorable John A Dix purchased Apple Hill, where Judge Nelson had first made his residence; but Mr. Dix, on removing to Albany at the time of his appointment as Adjutant-General of New York, sold this delightful place to Levi C. Turner, Esq. Judge Turner was born in Claremont, New Hampshire, pursued his studies at Dartmouth and Union Colleges, studied law with the Honorable E. B. Morehouse, of Cooperstown, and became a permanent resident of the village in 1827. Here he married a daughter of Robert Campbell, Esq., of Cooperstown. He was elected County Judge in 1855, and was again elected to the same office in 1859. He continued to pursue an honorable and distinguished professional career, in which he ever met with great success, until the period of his recent lamented decease.

The Honorable Schuyler Crippen, a native of Worcester, Otsego County, New York, where he resided and practiced law, removed to Cooperstown in 1830, and here continued in the successful prosecution of the labors of his profession for many years. In 1801, he was elected to the Bench of the Supreme Court of the State of New York, to fill the unexpired term, then four years, of the Honorable E. B. Morehouse, deceased.

Robert Campbell, Esq., whose name has been previously mentioned in these annals, had been known for the period of some forty-five years, as one of the ablest lawyers in the village of Cooperstown, and above all this, as an honest man – "the noblest work of God." Mr. Campbell was born in Cherry Valley in 1782. He pursued his studies and graduated at Union College, came to Cooperstown in 1802, and soon earned, by his professional labors as a lawyer, not less from the soundness of his views than from the marked integrity of his character, a distinguished place among the prominent lawyers of Otsego County; and he maintained this enviable position till his decease. Mr. Robert Campbell belonged to the very justly distinguished Campbell family of Cherry Valley. His brother, the Honorable James S. Campbell, previously named, is still living, being now in the 96th year of his age, and his mental faculties remain good, though his body gradually yields to the pressure of years, now filling nearly a century of time. The Campbell family had originally come from Scotland, in the early part of the eighteenth century. The Campbells, a name celebrated in history and song, trace back their genealogy over a thousand years, and belonged to the powerful clan of Argyle. Some years since, a nephew of Robert Campbell, the Honorable William W. Campbell, of Cherry Valley, visited the purple, heather-clad hills of the land of his ancestors. While making this sojourn in Scotland, the Celtic Society held its festival upon the lawn near the ancient castle of the Duke of Argyle; and its members gave to Mr. Campbell a true Scottish welcome. The President of the Society, in a beautiful address, stated that a wanderer from the ancestral flock had now returned to the land of his fathers, and was now among this gathering of his clan, and moved that he be elected an honorary member of the Society. This motion was enthusiastically carried by acclamation, the health of the new member drank with highland honors - each chieftain carrying his glass around his head with the right hand, repeating in Gaelic, "*Neish, neish, sheel ora, neish!*" - and then, the old Piper struck up the tune of the song of the clan at the meeting in 1745 - "*O, you're long in coming, but you're welcome.*"

The Campbell family, from the remote period of 1741, when Mr. James Campbell (the grandfather of Robert Campbell, Esq.) removed from Londonderry. New Hampshire, and with several of his *compagnons du voyage*, came to the vicinity of Cherry Valley, and here formed the pioneer settlement in this region, down to the present time, when this branch of the ancient clan, whose home had once been amid the far hills of Argyleshire, are now represented by such noble men as William W. Campbell, etc., have always maintained a prominent and justly distinguished position, alike in social and political relations, within Otsego County.

Among other gentlemen of considerable distinction, who have been residents of Cooperstown during longer or shorter periods. I may name Honorable George Morell, General Jacob Morris, Richard Cooper, Esq., etc. The reader has already inferred, from the names of distinguished families who have been referred to as residents of Cooperstown, that this pleasant rural village should possess an established and refined class of society. This has indeed been the fact from an early date in the settlement of the village, and it is now the only place, perhaps, among the country towns, whose inhabitants, or the more cultivated portion of them, possess those high moral and intellectual endowments, the virtuous principles and refined tastes which unite in forming true excellence of character, and by which individuals can properly, in their associated capacity, be recognized as society. For it will be clearly seen, that aside from this elevated standard which recognizes true womanhood and true manhood as constituted by nature, and unperverted by false education - the love of the beautiful, which is implanted in the mind of every individual fashion in the image of the Creator, and by which man is alone distinguished from the brutes, (for the animals all enjoy eating, drinking, sleeping, the warmth of their coats, locomotive, enjoyment of the senses, as well as man), and without mankind possessed this higher faculty, the divine attribute of communing with the true and beautiful, it need not be argued that it is just as impossible that they can be constituted as society, as it is for the brutes to be thus organized. The village of Cooperstown, in which many of the most worthy and accomplished families of our country have resided has always sustained an honorable pre-eminence in this respect: its society, alike in the pure tastes and exemplary associations which it has fostered, has ever aimed to be aristocrats - adopting as its only test the truthful, almost inspired words:

"A man's a man, for a' that."

This state of society, refined and of high moral tone, by which the village of Cooperstown stands so pre-eminently distinguished, is in striking contrast with that pretentious, sham aristocracy which starts up in every little village, as well as in cities, and which is composed of well-dressed fools, brainless fops, who can boast of a certain class of crimes and vicious indulgence, together with silly, simpering votaries of fashion, whose papas chance to have a pile of "Greenbacks" laid up - none of whom are intellectually, and certainly not morally, above the level of the brutes. It is this despicable, disgusting mushroom aristocratic society, which so justly excites the ridicule of all refined society, either of America or of Europe.

I have now only to trace one other interesting episode in the annals of Cooperstown. This rural village has been the home, not only of the illustrious jurists whose public career I have already imperfectly traced, but likewise of the great American novelist, - J. Fennimore Cooper, Esq., who occupied the front rank among the most eminent literary men of all lands and of all time, and whose imperishable works will carry the name of this village, where he resided, down to the remotest age in the roll of future time.

J. Fennimore Cooper was born on September 15, 1719, at Burlington, New Jersey. In October 1770, then between two and three years of age, he was brought by his parents to the vicinity of Otsego Lake, and his early boyhood years were passed in Cooperstown. It is said that he delighted in all manly sports, riding, shooting, fishing, skating, etc., and he found pleasurable excitement amid the wildwoods surrounding his highland home, or in trimming the sails or handling the oars of his boat upon the waters of the Otsego Lake. The active, impetuous, and generous boy is next sent to the school of Reverend Mr. Ellison, at Albany, where he made rapid progress, and at the early age of thirteen years, he was admitted to Yale College. Young Fennimore Cooper remained at college three years; then, obeying the impulses of his earnest, impetuous temperament, he went to sea, making his earliest voyage to England. In 1805, he entered the American navy, first in the capacity of midshipman, from which he was soon promoted to the office of Lieutenant. Cooper followed the sea for four years. In 1811, having previously resigned his position in the navy, Fennimore Cooper returned to New York, and marrying Miss Susan Delancy, they first made their home at Scarsdale, Westchester County, where Cooper found employment and pleasure in improving a farm, landscape gardening, and in literary pursuits. While here, he wrote the first chapter of his earliest novel, Precaution, mainly for his own amusement at the time, but reading it to his wile, she urged him to proceed with the story, which he, thus sanctioned by her approval, accordingly did. I believe this novel, the earliest literary production of his gifted pen, was published in 1820. This early work, though containing some blemishes, nevertheless gave brilliant promise of the surpassing genius and excellence that the author in after years so eminently evinced. This novel was quite favorably received in America and in Europe.

It was, almost the first among American books, very favorably reviewed by the English press. One publication, speaking of the new work, said: "Whoever may be the writer, we have to congratulate the public on the accession of a novelist possessing a peculiar felicity of talent for this species of composition." This novel appeared at an opportune time in regard to giving the name of our country a place in the literature of the world. England, and other nations of Europe, had hitherto denied that our country possessed any literary talent - a short time previous to the issue of Cooper's works, a prominent English review asking: "Who, in the four quarters of the globe, reads an American book?" J. Fennimore Cooper thus volunteered to assert, and to sustain by unanswerable proof, the reputation of his country in the world of letters; and which he afterwards continued to maintain by his genius and remarkable intellectual powers.

It may be said that the works of Cooper have been translated into a greater number of foreign languages than the writings of any other author, either of this or of foreign lands. The issue of his first novel *Precaution*, showed the earliest impulses in the genuine, vigorous existence of American literature. Wirt had written and published some able and fascinating productions. Charles Brockden Brown had also written several novels, as *Wielaud*, etc., which, although neglected by the reading world, still, in the mysterious gloom and interest which the author flung around these delineations of life amid the crowded streets of cities and thoroughfares of human existence, evinced an unusual order of talent. But the publication of Cooper's earlier tales was the first precursor to the brilliant and solid triumphs of American literature. It was about this period, the time when *Precaution*, and his second novel, *The Spy*, was published, (in 1820-21) - that several other meritorious works by American authors, as the *Sketch Book*, by Washington Irving; *The Idle Man*, by Richard Henry Dana, which continue among our classical works in prose, were issued; and in the same year that *The Spy* was sent to the press, in 1821, the first edition of poems by Fitz Greene Halleck, and also by William Cullen Bryant, were published - these poets, together with George D. Prentice, still maintaining their proud pre-eminence as the three most splendidly endowed, most eminent and illustrious poets of our own land- and now, when Byron, and Moore, and Scott, and Goethe have passed away, and no longer illuminate by the light of their genius the world of song - these three American authors, this immortal triumvirate, now hold the pre-eminent rank as the greatest and most distinguished poets of our age. The resplendent glory which their genius has flung around American literature, the luster which it has shed around the name of our country, however, has been amply sustained by the poetical productions of Miss Phebia Carey and Miss Alice Carey, and also by Willis, Dana, Bayard Taylor, T. B. Reade, Holmes, Whittier and Saxe.

And, in the fascinating department of literature where Cooper first led the way, and had acquired such wide and resplendent fame, such brilliant writers of fiction as Edgar Allen Poe, Nathaniel Hawthorne, Miss H. E. Prescott, Herman Melville, George William Curtis, John P. Kennedy, W. G. Sims, and R. H. Dana, Jr. have labored with eminent success, and won the enduring laurels of fame.

In the department of historical writing, the great and illustrious historian, George Bancroft, Esq., justly occupies the most eminent position; and, in the unequalled value of his material, and the elaborate manner in which his comprehensive genius has given it shape in rearing the immortal temple of American history, he stands alone in the unrivalled grandeur of his intellect unapproached and unapproachable, and he has nobly earned the laurels of enduring fame, has won the lofty pre-eminence as the ablest and most illustrious historian of our age, not less than of all time.

I am aware that there are many who object to the particular department of writing that J. Fennimore Cooper has chosen, because it is mainly fiction-romance; but I can well say, that so far as my own researches have extended, his several tales whose scenes are laid within the section of central New York, as *The Spy, Pioneers, Last of the Mohicans, Path Finder, Deer Slayer*, etc., more truthfully illustrate our early history, when the Red Man and the pioneer shared in the occupation of our country, and better describes the character of either the Indian, or the hardy emigrant, than is done in any of the professed histories, or narratives of events transacted in this region - perhaps excepting the very reliable work written by Mr. Campbell, the *Annals of Tryon County*.

In fact, the early years of Cooper's life, which were passed amid the wilds of Otsego, in frequent association with the aboriginal occupants of the forest, and the rough settlers here and there found amid the new clearings, had furnished the material from which his genius, like some fairy *Ariel*, so faithfully reproduced' the exact images and pictures of pioneer life, and so faithfully delineated the real characteristics of both the red man and the primitive settler. He has truthfully delineated human life as it actually existed," and has accurately described the picturesque scenery of this region of the state, the vicinity of Otsego Lake and the Susquehanna; and it is certainly not material that the novelist should have adopted, in designating the various persons represented in his narratives by the precise names of living individuals.

It is asserted that Enoch Crosby, who lived at southeast Dutchess County, (now Putnam County) at the time of the Revolution, was the individual from whom Cooper drew the fictitious character of Harvey Birch, in *The Spy*; and Timothy Murphy, the Virginia rifleman, whose unerring aim had sent the bullet which terminated the life of General Frazier, at Saratoga - formed the original of one of the characters represented in Cooper's works; while Shipman, the hunter and fisherman of the Otsego region, was the real individual from whom the masterly delineation of Leatherstocking is drawn.

The novelist has faithfully described real life; and he has clothed his narratives with not more of the gorgeous coloring of romance than actual lite very frequently gives to the changing scenes which we encounter, not more of romance than many, those indeed who have a soul capable of the emotions of passion, realize in their daily existence. And the delineation of the passion of love has held its spell over the pen of the novelist and poet, and held in its enchantment the interest of the reader, from the earliest era of human existence, and will continue thus to assert its power while time shall endure. The passion of love, while it is the most intense and absorbing sentiment which can actuate the human breast, is, at the same time, one of the purest and holiest, in its impulses and aspirations, which can thrill the bosom; it is a sentiment, a feeling, which is always pure - although it becomes so often improperly confounded with a debased animal appetite, to which it is as unlike and far removed as paradise from Pluto's realm.

It is sometimes objected, that the persons represented in these stories are placed in situations which they might use for wrongful purpose; but, I should imagine that little confidence should be placed in the virtuous principles of those who refrained from vice simply because no opportunity presented for its indulgence. The pure in heart will remain pure, and stainless of sin, under whatever circumstances they may be placed.

The delineations of the passion of love, given by Cooper, are drawn with a masterly hand, are drawn from nature and from life. Over the fascination pages where he describes Mabel Dunham, Elizabeth Temple, etc., etc., over the romantic episodes woven amid these heroines - the fair maiden long will linger, with glowing and wildly-beating heart, until she pillows her soft cheek upon these enchanting pages in slumber, but with her dreams, bathed with love's rosy light, only to return and dwell amid the fairy scenes described in these volumes. Perhaps no other author has so truthfully delineated the noble sentiment of friendship, as it sometimes exists in real life; nor, in all the range of fiction, can there be found a character, more original in its conception, in its delineation or masterly noble, generous, and pure, in the qualities with which it is invested, than the Leatherstocking- a character which the rare genius of the novelist has successfully, and with constantly increasing interest, carried through five different stories, *The Pioneers, The Last of the Mohicans,*

The Prairie, The Pathfinders, and *The Deer Slayer.*

In Cooper's first romance of the sea, *The Pilot,* the character of Tom Coffin, and also of Bolthorpe, are drawn with scarcely less vigor than his finest touches of pioneer life. In his various tales of the sea, *The Pilot, Red Hover, Two Admirals, Wing-and-Wing, Afloat and Ashore, The Water Witch,* etc., which are illustrated with the bold and striking imagery borrowed from his own adventurous life upon the ocean for six years, he has given inimitable descriptions of the beauty and grandeur which haunts the sea, and truthfully described the romantic career of the hardy, generous seamen. In the class of his novels relating to the sea, Cooper has no rival.

I cannot dwell upon the various novels of this great author. Commencing with the publication of *Precaution,* in 1820, and terminating with the *Ways of the Hour,* in 1850, including in this time the production of thirty-nine different tales, all of them marked by strong originality, and the larger portion bearing the impress of unequalled genius and intellectual power.

The residence of J. Fennimore Cooper, in Westchester County, after his marriage continued for some length of time. He then removed to Cooperstown, and passed several years upon his place near the beautiful Otsego Lake ; and about the year 1818, he removed, with his family, to New York city, and while there, associated with the most eminent men of the nation, as Chancellor Kent, Durand, whose name has been rendered illustrious as the first artist of our age; President King, of Columbia College, Verplanck, Bryant and Halleck, who then, as now, ranked as the first poets of our land, etc.

In 1826, the year in which the *Last of the Mohicans* was published, Cooper went with his family to Europe, and made his residence for some time in Paris, where he associated upon terms of intimate friendship with the Marquis de La Fayette, und other distinguished men of France.

In 1833 after a sojourn of seven years in various countries of Europe, but residing principally in France, Cooper returned to the United States. He afterwards published a series of graphic and interesting sketches relating to the various countries in Europe that he had visited, in a work of eight volumes. Soon after his return from Europe, Cooper made his permanent home in the village of Cooperstown, at the old family residence - the Hall - upon the Southern border of the Otsego Lake. Here he employed his lime in literary pursuits, generally writing during the earlier portion of the day, and in agricultural employments.

The mind of Cooper was fond of solitude, and he was very rarely seen in the crowded streets or in places of public resort, for he preferred to have the indulgence of his own meditations. The man of genius is never alone, for at his bidding the air is thronged with fairy shapes, with angelic beings many and beautiful. Thus the great novelist passed his time in the quiet seclusion of the home circle, or in rambling amid the solitary woods which bordered the lovely Otsego Lake, and in these lonely hours gathering the thoughts, the inspirations, which he afterwards infused into his works, and which should electrify and hold spell-bound with their potent charms the minds of millions throughout the wide globe.

This love of retirement and solitude seems to be a peculiar characteristic of great and capacious intellects, as, for instance. Lord Byron and Daniel Webster - both of these remarkable men passing most of their leisure hours alone amid the grandeur of mountain solitude in solitary musings by the side of the magnificent and mighty ocean.

While residing near Otsego Lake, Cooper continued his literary labors, writing his sketches and novels. From the earnest attachment which he felt for this pursuit, and the pleasure that he derived from it, with such a mind as he possessed, when thus engaged in literary effort, and with every nerve of his being thrilled with intensest emotion, and pleasure, he enjoyed in a single hour a greater amount of happiness -- more of the real, exhilarating pleasure of life than millionaires can possibly do in the entire course of their sordid existence.

Cooper had become possessed of a moderate amount of means from his father's estate; but fortunately he relied upon his own resources of mind and active exertions, while in early life, and his manly character, his earnest, robust feelings and sensibilities were thus developed and matured. The illustrious German poet Goethe has very truthfully remarked that it was the great misfortune of Lord Byron that he inherited the wealth connected with his peerage. Large riches certainly never benefitted any man, but have the invariable effect of destroying all healthy and generous impulses of the human bosom.

Cooper was a man of earnest, positive nature and temperament, impulsive and decided in his convictions, of robust feelings and warm affections-- sincere and plain in his likes and dislikes, and abhorring all disguise, he was always frank in the expression of his opinions.

He had the manliness and courage to lead a true and honest life, governed by strict moral principles and devout religious sentiment - and hence it will not be surprising, that in these times when it is necessary that a person commit some crime in order to become popular with the crowd, that Cooper had to battle with such bitter and malicious enmity. But in all past time, as now, the noble, self-sacrificing martyr who gives the efforts and labors of his life to advance the happiness of man- kind, must be content to wear the crown of thorns, ere his brow can be twined with the wreath of laurel, the immortal crown of fame whose leaves shall continue ever fadeless, and fresh in their beauty through the long-elapsing years of eternal time.

Cooper, like all other men of great intellect and great soul, had his faults. But, a man should be judged by what he actually possesses by the virtues of his character, rather than by its deficiencies or defeats. History, indeed, has ever shown, that the man possessing the greatest endowment of talent and the greatest virtues, have also the greatest faults, the strongest passions- blending in their character, and requiring control. And is it not to teach us that among all the exalted beings that have appeared upon earth, one alone has been faultless - that Jesus Christ, among all who have worn the human form upon earth, should be reverenced and worshipped as God.

Cooper is now gone. He has passed away forever. During the year 1861, his health, which had continued robust up to this period, began to fail. In April 1851, the distinguished physician. Dr. J. W. Francis, had been consulted in regard to the alarming symptoms which were presented, but Cooper's physical frame continued still further to yield to the influence of disease through the summer months, that to him were now bringing their fragrance and bloom as the last offering which they might give. He was surrounded by a kind and affectionate family among whom was his gifted and accomplished daughter, the authoress of *Rural Hours,* Miss Susan J. Cooper. Thus surrounded by all that affection could ask, and cheered by the divine consolations of religion, on a calm Sabbath day, September 14, 1851, J. Fennimore Cooper departed this mortal life.

As the sad intelligence of the decease of the great man who had long occupied so large a space in the public mind, so long been one of the brightest ornaments of our literature, passed over our land, it filled the country with mourning. Various public meetings were held, expressive of the general grief; among them, one of the largest and most impressive in its character, assembled at Metropolitan Hall, New York, on the evening of February 25, 1852. This meeting was composed of the ablest and most illustrious men of all our land. Irving and Bancroft, and Curtis were there. Daniel Webster, the great New England statesman, was called to preside over this unusual assemblage, and delivered, on taking the chair, an appropriate and eloquent address; while the great and distinguished poet, William Cullen Bryant, pronounced a discourse commemorative of the life and character of the lamented Fennimore Cooper. And concerning this oration, I can only say, that it was a worthy and fitting tribute to the career of the illustrious deceased.

The flowers which spring up and cover the graves of the departed, also cover the remembrance of their frailties- while all that had claimed our love in the living character of the lamented dead shall go down to claim the admiration of posterity. So long as exalted genius, nobleness of soul, and purity of moral character shall command the admiration and sway the impulses of the human heart, that illustrious name, J. Fennimore Cooper, will be honored, and reverenced and loved.

CHAPTER VI

In returning to the region of Newtown, I will pause one moment at Tioga Point - and briefly refer to the council that was held at this place in November 1790. This council, I find, was called because of the murder of two of the Senecas on Pine Creek, and to settle the difficulty. Colonel Timothy Pickering who then resided at Wyoming, represented the U. S. Government.

The council commenced on November 16, and continued until the 23rd of that same month. The famous Mohican chief, Hendrick Aupaumet who had received a classical education at Princeton, New Jersey, and was captain of a band of Housatonic Indians in the Revolutionary War: he afterwards lived near Catharine's Town, and was taken care of during his last illness, about the year 1798, by Mr. Thomas Nichols, and buried near a huckleberry swamp lying upon the east side of the present village of Havana, New York); - with Red Jacket (Sa-go-ye-wa-tha) Farmer's Brother (Ho-nai-ye-wus), and Fish-Carrier (O-jea-geh-ta) who was a distinguished warrior of the Cayugas.

The Indians came to this council very much excited, and were still further exasperated and inflamed by the eloquent, artful speech of Red Jacket. This chief who now first acquired distinction as an orator, brought up the controversy between the Iroquois and Phelps & Gorham, relative to the sale of the lands of the Six Nations, at Fort Stanwix in October 1784. However, Colonel Pickering succeeded in quieting the difficulty.

In December of 1790 in which this council met at Tioga, a deputation of the Six Nations met at Philadelphia, to remonstrate against the treaty made at Fort Stanwix, which was still existent; and the chiefs here invoked the aid of General Washington, whom they termed Hanondaganius, to arrange the affair. A note, signed by General Knox, Secretary of War, December 20, 1791, says: "The Corn-Planter, a war captain of the Senecas, and other Indians of the same tribe, being in Philadelphia, in December 1790, measures were taken to induce their interference with the Western tribes to prevent further hostilities, and an arrangement was made that Corn-Planter should accompany Colonel Thomas Proctor on a visit to the Miami villages, for that purpose.

Further, measures were taken in April 1791, to draw the Six Nations to a conference at a distance from the theatre of war, and Colonel Pickering was appointed to hold the conference. It was decided to be held at Painted Post, on June 17, 1791; but from the papers returned to the War Department, it seems to have been held at Newtown Point.

Many early pioneers in the Chemung Valley had distinctly remembered circumstances connected with this Council. The Indians who had assembled to kindle the council-fire here, in great numbers, were encamped along the western part of Newtown, their tents ranging from the place where the Brainard House now stands, to the upper portion of the present city of Elmira.

Among the early pioneers in the Chemung Valley who were present at this Council were Matthias Hollenback, Elisha Lee, Eleazer Lindley, and William Jenkins. The treaty was negotiated beneath the shade of a tree, which afterwards became known as the "Old Council Tree." It had stood on the spot, now near the corner of Cross and Conongue streets, upon the lot at present occupied by Mr. Hector Seward, and the tree remained standing until a recent time, when it was cut down by Mr.

Seward. This council of 1791- the treaty formed at Newtown - at which Colonel Timothy Pickering, in behalf of the United States, and Corn-Planter (Gai-ant-wake) and Red Jacket, with other eminent sachems of the Iroquois, were present, and engaged in the discussions around the council-fire - indeed holds a memorable place in history. It was at this council that Red Jacket had shown those remarkable powers, by which he afterward held such complete supremacy over the Senecas, and became the leading or dominant chief in that tribe.

I may add that Timothy Pickering, Esq., who represented the American Government here, possessed great powers of persuasion, while he had acquired the tact of exerting a remarkable influence over the Indians, by which he was enabled successfully to conclude this treaty at Newtown. Colonel Pickering, in command of a body of men at Salem, Massachusetts in February 1795, was among the earliest of the patriots at that period to oppose, by force, British invasion. At the time of the battle of Lexington, marching with his regiment to intercept the enemy, during Washington's campaign in New Jersey, Pickering was associated with the Commander-in-chief in the perilous conflicts of that period, holding the rank, and position of Adjutant-General. In 1780, he held the appointment of Quartermaster-General. In connection with Washington's administration, Colonel Pickering received appointment as Postmaster-General, in 1791, and upon the resignation of General Knox as Secretary of War, he was assigned that position, which he occupied until 1795, when President Washington appointed him Secretary of State, which he held until the close of Washington's administration in 1800. Mr. Pickering was chosen United States Senator from his native State, Massachusetts, in 1803, and again in 1805. He died at Salem, in 1829, aged eighty-seven years.

At a distance of some two miles west of Elmira, is an eminence, known as Fort Hill, and where can be traced the remains of a fortification. This eminence is upon the north side of the Chemung River, while the opposite side is bordered by a deep ravine- forming a precipitous headland. An embankment, some fourteen or fifteen feet wide at its base, and three feet in elevation, extends from the brow of the ravine in a Northern direction to the summit of the bank resting upon the river, and is some two hundred feet in length. This artificial wall of earth has an outer ditch, with two slight trenches, running parallel with the ancient bastion across the entire width of this bold eminence. This earthwork, undoubtedly constructed for warlike purposes; however, presents an appearance indicating a more recent construction than the *Ancient Works of Western New York*, which the writer of this sketch had surveyed in the year 1850, under authority of the Regents of the University of the State of New York.

This entrenchment near Elmira occupies an admirable position for defense, as it is only accessible from a single direction, a military engineer would not have evinced greater strategic art in the construction of this defensive earthwork. The fortification here may have been, probably, reared by the Iroquois during the period of early French expeditions into the territory of the Six Nations. I may here remark that while prosecuting these researches relative to the history of this valley, I received information of an extensive series of ancient earthworks located upon the tributary streams of the Susquehanna and the Delaware, while it is known that many Indian mounds, etc., are situated in other portions of the State. It is only through a complete survey of these fast-perishing memorials of former empire, these rapidly decaying monuments which now afford the only record of that race that once occupied and held sovereignty of our soil, by a rigid investigation, and scientific research of the entire subject, in its archaeological, ethnological, and historical relations, that we may hope to be able to rescue an instructive chapter in the annals of the past from oblivion, or cast any light upon the history of the State during its occupancy by the mound-builders - while possibly such an exploration might unravel the mystery regarding their origin and fate, and be the means of perpetuating, before these ancient mounds and earthworks are all effaced, some reliable record of the Ante-Columbian period in the history of our land.

I will now attempt to give a brief review of the Iroquois occupation of the region embraced in these historical enquiries.

Jefferson, whose philosophical mind gave profound investigations to nearly every department of human knowledge, in his *Notes on Virginia*, in giving the list of the Indian tribes, their location and. numbers, in 1779, make the following statement: "Cayugas on the Cayuga Lake and near branch of Susquehanna, 220; Senecas, on the waters of the Susquehanna, Ontario, on the head of Ohio, 650." The portion of the Indian tribes who inhabited the valley, and ranged the adjoining hills, between the Chemung River and Seneca Lake, at the time of Sullivan's expedition, were principally Cayugus, Tuscarora, and Senecas. The Indian king, Canadesaga, of the Senecas, was killed at the Battle of Chemung. This region was common hunting ground to all the Six Nations. When it began to be settled by emigrants from the East, in 1758, large numbers of Indians still resided between the lake and the river. It was at this period, when the Iroquois councils were graced by the presence of so many distinguished chiefs, that Red Jacket began to acquire and exercise his unrivaled ascendency among the Iroquois.

I will here make in extract from a M.SS. of the late Honorable Thomas Maxwell who had held the rank and exercised the authority of a Sachem among the Senecas, in which he thus refers to Red Jacket, etc.: "The once haughty Iroquois has withdrawn to a quiet spot on the western skirts of his lordly patrimony. He no longer, as in the days of his power, holds the olive branch in one hand, and the tomahawk in the other, to sway the decisions of councils. They have produced many distinguished men.

Among these none were more eminent than the celebrated Red Jacket. He exhibited great powers of oratory at the Treaty, held by Colonel Pickering at Newtown Point, in 1791.

Red Jacket who had always opposed all attempts to civilize or Christianize the tribes, exhibited on this occasion his greatest powers of mind, in opposition to the proposals of the government; and the result, was, they were only, accepted by Corn-Planter's tribe. In a conversation held with Red Jacket, at Bath, New York, in 1828, he informed me that when a child, he was present at a great Council-Fire of the Tribes, at Shenandoah, Virginia. The various nations were represented by their most distinguished orators, but the greatest among them was Logan, a Cayuga who had removed from his residence on the Cayuga to Shamokin, Pennsylvania, on the Susquehanna. Red Jacket remarked that he was so highly delighted with Logan's eloquence, that he resolved to devote himself to public speaking and following Logan as his model. He said that he was in the habit of speaking in the woods where he could find a waterfall, where he exercised his voice amid the roaring waters, to acquire the necessary command and tone to address large assemblies. One of his favorite resorts for this purpose was the magnificent waterfall at Havana [Montour Falls]. The name of the stream was She-qua-gah or, as he interpreted it, "the place of the roaring waters."

The waterfall seems to have been his peculiar inspiration. In early life the beautiful She-qua-gah, and in his mature years the mighty Ne-auga-rah (I give his own pronunciation.) were his favorite haunts. There are certain qualities of mind exhibited in the untutored Indian, which shine forth in all the luster of natural perfection. His simple integrity, his generosity, his imbounded hospitality, his love of truth, and his unwavering fidelity, are graces of humanity which neither education can impart, nor civilization confer; and when they exist, it is that the gifts, of deity have never been perverted.

    The writer of this sketch, too, has had some opportunity to become conversant with Indian life. He has sojourned for weeks, when he had not seen civilized man, amidst the rude children of the forest, he has lain down to secure repose in the night-camp of the Indian, around the tire which they had kindled in the wildwoods- he has accompanied the Indian hunter upon the chase, and has been guided by the Indian maiden through the pathless forest- and can most fully reiterate the opinion regarding the prevailing features of the Indian character expressed in the manuscript from which I have above quoted; and in fearless, frank honesty of purpose, in genuine, unpretending nobleness, of feeling, in the abiding love and worship which he clings to the sacred associations and memories of the past, and in abiding friendship manifested by one sex, - the natural, unostentatious, but real chastity and virtue, and evinced by the other sex - I, can only say, that the Indian character presents, in these respects, a model which "cultivated society" might well choose for emulation.

    Among all the barbaric tribes, the Haudenosaunee, or "People of the Long House," the Iroquois - held pre-eminent rank for eloquence, bravery, and skill in war – consummate address and energy in perfecting all the arts which gave success to Indian policy. But, the mighty league that once held sovereignty of all these lands watered by the Susquehanna and its tributary streams, has lost its supremacy forever! Atatasho and Hiawatha, the deities of this Confederacy, no longer worshipped upon the backs of these noble rivers, have departed. The council-fires of the Iroquois, once marking their wide jurisdiction, have been extinguished. Their empire has passed away; and the shadows of nights, which have already enveloped so many Indian nations, now gathers darkly around the few remaining Iroquois who yet linger here, where the gleam of the setting sun dimly falls upon the graves of their fathers, to lament the departed greatness of their once powerful empire, and ere long its impenetrable gloom will wrap even this small remnant of the once haughty Iroquois in darkness and oblivion.

I will now attempt to gather, and briefly narrate such reminiscences as may yet remain about the early settlement and history of Newtown. Colonel John Hendy was the pioneer of the Chemung Valley. He came to Newtown in 1786. Colonel Hendy was a veteran of the Revolution, being engaged, at the age of nineteen, at the Battle of Princeton, and at Trenton. Before reaching the age of twenty-one he was commissioned as Captain and participated in the battle of Monmouth, and in a brilliant manner brought off the remnant of his company from the field. It was here that Captain Hendy had gallantly borne to a place of safety the brave General Mercer who was wounded during the action and survived only a few days.

Colonel Hendy had broken with the plough the first field, and raised the first crop of grain in the Chemung Valley. He was appointed the captain of a militia company by Governor George Clinton, on February 22, 1789, in the town of Chemung, County of Montgomery; and commissioned second Major of a Regiment of Militia in the county of Tioga, whereof Thomas Baldwin is Lieutenant-Colonel commandant, on March 22, 1797, by Governor Jay; and commissioned as Lieutenant-Colonel in 1803, by Governor George Clinton.

The predecessor of Colonel Thomas Baldwin in command of the regiment earlier mentioned was an ensign in Sullivan's army, at the Battle of Chemung, August 31, 1779. Colonel Hendy was born in Northumberland County, Pennsylvania, on September 2, 1757. He emigrated from Elmira to the west. That is the latest record that I find of this gallant veteran of the War of Independence, and hardy pioneer of the Chemung Valley.

Guy Maxwell, Esq., had emigrated to the Chemung Valley September 1788. He was second son of Alexander Maxwell, of Claverock, England; and his mother, whose name before her marriage was Jane McBratney, was reputed as a lady of rare accomplishments, and was connected with the "clan McPherson." They embarked from a port in Scotland for America in June 1770, but were shipwrecked in the Irish Channel, upon the coast of Ireland, where, on July 15, 1770, Guy Maxwell was born. The family, upon its arrival in America, settled in Virginia. Guy Maxwell came to this valley in 1788, and first settled at Tioga Point, where he remained until 1759, when he removed to Newtown [Elmira]. His house, a frame dwelling 32 by 23 feet in size upon the ground, was on Water Street.

Newtown was originally planned out on a lot granted to Jeffrey Wisner, lying on Newtown Creek. The first buildings were erected in 1790, at a place now known as Sullivan Street. The dwelling houses of Dr. Hinchman, Dr. Scott, Peter Loop and Christian Loop were built on Sullivan Street.

In December, 1794, Guy Maxwell, of Tioga Point, and S. Hepburn had purchased of Mr. T. White a parcel of land in lot 195, containing 100 acres, for five hundred pounds, and laid out a village plot on the bank of Chemung River. In the conveyance this plot was designated DeWittsburg, but the place continued to be known as Newtown until 1811, when it was changed to Elmira by an Act of the New York Legislature.

The town of Chemung was laid out in 1788 by James Clinton, John Hathorn and John Cantine, Commissioners, and a map of the town deposited in the office of the Secretary of State for New York. These commissioners had surveyed, here, October 1788, lots lying in the town of Chemung, and situated near the Tioga, or Chemung River, for the several individuals below named: Israel Parshall, 209 acres; Usual Bates, 183 acres; C. Christ, 162 acres; Josiah Green, 400 acres; Richard Edsell, 2d, 285 acres. They also surveyed a lot of 450 acres for John Miller, in Big Flats.

In 1778, Guy Maxwell was appointed Principal Assessor for the Sixth Assessment District of the Ninth Division of the State of New York, which comprised Tioga County, which then included six towns, viz: Newtown, Chemung, Owego, Chenango, Union and Jericho. This assessment was made in pursuance of an act levying a direct tax, under the administration of President John Adams. Colonel Nicolas Fish, of New York, was the Supervisor of Revenue for the State of New York. The original M.SS. (now lying before me) of the assessment roll of the Sixth District, containing names of the inhabitants, etc., is dated October 1, 1778. Soon after this assessment was made, Mr. Maxwell was appointed Sheriff of Tioga County, by Governor George Clinton. Guy Maxwell was a soldier in the Revolutionary War. He died in 1814.

Among the pioneers who had settled about Newtown, I will mention the names of Matthias Hollenback, formerly of Wyoming, Pennsylvania who resided upon Water Street, in a house built partly frame and partly of logs, size 29 by 20 feet. John Konkle, a veteran of the Revolution who lived in a frame house, 20 by 16 feet, on Water Street, and who died at the age of seventy years. Joseph Hincherman, M.D. who had been a soldier of the Revolution, and was sheriff of Tioga County from 1795 to 1799, living in a frame dwelling-house, 38 by 30 feet; he died in 1802, at the age of forty years. Selah Matthews who lived in a frame house on the east side of Main (now Sullivan) Street, and who was a veteran of the Revolutionary War, dying in 1833, at the age of seventy-one years. Peter Loop who had erected a frame-house 22 by 18 feet, on Main Street mentioned above. John Stower who built a house of hewn logs, 34 by 20 feet, on the east side of Main Street. Cornelius Lowe who lived in a log-house, 28 by 22 feet in size, with kitchen 18 by 22 feet, on Water Street, where Lyman Covell has resided of late years. Lemuel Churchill who built a house of square logs, 18 by 16 feet, on the east side of Main Street. Christian Scott who had erected a frame dwelling house, 28 by 20 feet, also on Main street. John Miller who lived in a house 34 by 17 feet, J. Brown who lived in a log-house 23 by 21 feet, erected on Water Street. Robert Starrett kept the tavern which was on Water Street, and was a frame building, 30 by 30 feet in size, with kitchen 18 by 20 feet, and which was afterward known as the Kline House. These were the settler's thus living in their frame and log dwellings, about the village in 1798.

 The haze and darkness that has been gathering through the long night of the past, and which had nearly enveloped the homes, as they once existed, of the pioneers, is here withdrawn, and we again have a glimpse of Newtown, as it had stood in the period of its early settlement - an accurate though rude picture of this rural hamlet by the river side, as it appeared sixty-nine years ago.

 Beside the pioneers who were living at Newtown as above mentioned, in 1798, at this early period, the pioneers below named had also settled in the region about Newtown and within the present limits of Chemung County. Colonel John Hendy who in the year 1796 had made the first settlement in Chemung Valley. Honorable Vincent Mathews who was a member of Assembly in the New York State Legislature in 1794-95, and was the first Senator elected from the Western District to the State Legislature, thus early occupying position in the Senate from 1796 to 1802, and, also a representative in Congress in 1809-1811. Brinton Paine, an officer of the Army in the Revolution, and who had been taken prisoner during the war and confined in a British prison-ship; he resided here for many years, and died at the advanced age of eighty- one years. Reverend Roswell Goff who organized the first church, or religious society (Baptist) which was established in Chemung Valley, formed in 1790, at Wellsburg, New York. Joseph Hiller, Isaac Baldwin, James Bower, John Hendy, Henry Baldwin, Caleb Baker, E. Bennett, and Elijah Brick who had commenced a settlement at Brickville, in 1798, where he was soon followed by Captain D. McDowell and William Wyncoop.

The house of William Dunn, and that of Nathaniel W. Howell, were on the bank of the river, east of Sullivan Street. Many old houses, erected during the early period of the settlement of Newtown, in the neighborhood of Sullivan Street, are yet remaining. In these buildings, where moss is now cropping round the crumbling door-sill, and over the shattered windowpane, the early settlers had lived and had their share of joy and of sorrow - here, too, they loved, and had been actors in romances as impassioned and as strange, perchance, as any that are recorded in our literature. But, these early residents have all passed away and are silent within the tomb, as we, too, ere long, shall be.

The first courthouse at Newtown, or Elmira, was erected about 1796, on Main (now Sullivan) Street, near its intersection with Cross Street. It was a two-story building, constructed of logs. Within the walls of that old courthouse have sat such eminent jurists as Livingston, Spencer, Kent, Van Ness, Woodworth, Tompkins, etc. And within its rude bar have been uttered the eloquent arguments of such distinguished lawyers as Hornell, Matthews, Haight, Sedgwick, Avery, Spencer, Dickinson, Diven and Collier.

The judges on the Courts of Tioga County were: Abraham Miller, from 1779 to 1798; John Patterson, from 1798 to 1807; John Miller, from 1807 to 1800; E. Coryell, from 1810 to 1818; G. W. Barstow, from 1818 to 1828; Grant B. Baldwin, from 1828 to 1833; and John R. Drake, from 1833 to 1838.

William Dunn who had been a soldier in the Revolutionary War, and who had made his residence at Newtown, died here at the age of ninety years.

I may here remark that in 1797 Newtown was visited by the Duke of Orleans- Louis Philippe. The father of this celebrated exile had perished on the scaffold, and his brothers, the Duke de Mountsponsier and the Count de Beaujolais, had been imprisoned in the Castle of St. Jean, at Marseilles. However, in 1700, the French Directory released the prisoners of State, on the condition that they should repair to the United States, accompanied by the Duke of Orleans. They reached Philadelphia in the winter of 1776, and remained there until spring, when they visited Washington at Mount Vernon. Thence they traveled through several western states, and arrived at Buffalo, New York in June; and thence proceeded to Canandaigua, Geneva, and Havana. From Havana, the royal exiles went to Elmira, on foot. They had letters of introduction from Thomas Morris, of Canandaigua to several leading citizens at Newtown, or Elmira.

The Duke of Orleans, and his companions, stopped, while at Newtown, at the Kline House (earlier described in this sketch), and remained hero some ten days. During their sojourn, they were engaged in fishing, hunting, etc. A Mr. John Stower, at Newtown, furnished the exiles with a durham boat, in which they descended the Susquehanna to Wilkes-Barre, and then went across the country to Philadelphia.

Some years later, Newtown was visited by another exile - Louis Napoleon - while this distinguished exile was engaged in his travels through our country. He is described by residents of this section who had seen him while staying here, to have been an athletic, energetic man. He was a relative, and I may add, a worthy representative of the Great Emperor, Napoleon - who was, indeed, the great master in the realm of human action, as Shakespeare was the great master in the realm of human thought.

Louis Napoleon, while at Newtown, had stopped, I have been informed, at the Kline House - the same rude tavern where Louis Philippe had earlier stayed. The traveler who now, in humble guise, had put up at this log-tavern, near the river bank, affords a striking contrast with the magnificence which waits upon the Imperial monarch of the Tuileries- the Emperor Napoleon III - acknowledged to be the ablest and wisest ruler now holding power upon earth. And yet, such are life's strange contrasts. Burns, the poor, despised writer of song, actually dying from the effects of want and neglect (as I have been informed by relatives of Burns, living at Ayr) - but the time has already come when even the name of Scotland is remembered mainly because it had been the home of Robert Burns!

I have earlier referred to the first church organized in this region in 1790, by Reverend Roswell Goff. The first Presbyterian Church at Newtown was organized in 1793. Its earliest pastor was Reverend Daniel Thatcher. A second Presbyterian Church was organized in 1860, of which the first pastor was Reverend D. Murdoch. The first Baptist Church was organized in May 1829 - its pastor, was Reverend P. G. Gillett. Trinity Church, Episcopal, was organized in 1833 - its first rector was Reverend Thomas Clarke. Independent Church, organized in 1845 - its first pastor, Reverend F. W. Gravers.

The various churches exercise a wide influence for good; and yet it should be wished that their communicants sustained a closer relation to the religion taught by our Divine Savior, Jesus Christ, and which had been exemplified by his followers by entire renouncement of self by their love to God and to man, and in leading a pure and virtuous life.

Colonel Matthias Hollenback from Wilkes-Barre, Pennsylvania was the earliest merchant at Newtown. His store was at the junction of the [Newtown] Creek with the Chemung River. S. Tuttle and R. Covell commenced mercantile business in Newtown, in 1807, which was successfully continued during many years. Guy Maxwell, Esq., Thomas Goldsborough, T. M. Perry, J. Erwin, E. Heller, L. Covell, M. Covell, J. Baldwin, J. Cherry, J. Hollenback, Thomas Maxwell, Samuel H. Maxwell, and J. Reynolds were also among the early merchants at Elmira.

The early lawyers at Elmira who had acquired any forensic distinction, may be thus named: Peter Loop, D. Jones, Vincent Matthews, S. H. Haight, George C. Edwards, J. Robinson, Aaron Rankle, T. North, William Maxwell, Thomas Maxwell, A. S. Diven, A. S. Thurston, S. G. Mathews, &c.

The early physicians at Newtown or Elmira, may be thus enumerated: Joseph Hinchman, Amos Peck, C. Scott, J. Chamberlain, John Ross. James Ross, A. G. White, Dr. Aspenwall, J. Purdy, T. Brooks and R. Bancroft. These men, the early merchants, lawyers, and physicians of Newtown, are now nearly all deceased. A few yet remain - the honored representatives of that class whose enterprise, learning and skill, had contributed so much to advance Elmira in prosperity, commercial position, and reputation, to the proud rank which this city now claims and occupies.

Among the leading men of Elmira whom I have above referred to, none are entitled to claim a higher rank in the esteem of posterity than the Maxwells - Honorable William Maxwell and Honorable Thomas Maxwell - who were sons of Guy Maxwell.

William Maxwell was born at Tioga Point [Athens], Pennsylvania, February 11, 1894. He represented the Tioga County in the Assembly of the State Legislature of New York, in 1828. In 1846, he was the delegate from Chemung County in the Convention held to amend the Constitution of the State of New York, and was the first member of Assembly elected from Chemung County after the new Constitution of 1846 wont into effect. He died at the age of sixty-two, ripe in years and honors.

The Honorable Thomas Maxwell was indeed widely known and distinguished for his marked ability, sound, practical judgment and unswerving integrity, evinced in public not less than in private life. He was honored with important trusts, bestowed by his fellow citizens. He held the office of County Clerk from March 1819), to January 1829; and was a Representative in Congress from Tioga, in 1829-31. He departed this life several years since, widely and deeply mourned.

The early members of the State Legislature - the Assembly of New York, from Tioga County, which then embraced Newtown, were: John Fitch, 1792; John Patterson, 1793; Vincent Mathews, 1791-95; Emanuel Coryell, in 1796-97; E. Coryell and Benjamin Harvey, in 1798.

James McMasters was the first sheriff of Tioga County, and held this office from 1791 to 1795; Joseph Hinchman, M. D., was the sheriff of the County, from 1791 to 1799; Edward Edwards was appointed Sheriff in 1799, but only held this office until 1800, and was then succeeded by Guy Maxwell who remained in this position, and exercised the duties of sheriff of the county, until 1804.

This section, the region about Newtown, had been represented in the State Senate by Vincent Mathews, from 1796 to 1892, and also by other distinguished men, here named, viz: G. W. Barstow, from 1819 to 1822; J.G. McDowell, from 1823 to 1835; and D. S. Dickinson, from 1840 to 1844.

Among the Representatives in Congress from this District, which embraced Newtown (or Elmira), the able and distinguished men below mentioned had resided at this village: Honorable Vincent Mathews, Honorable Thomas Maxwell, Honorable Samuel Partridge who was a member of Congress in 1841-43; and Honorable Hiram Gray who represented the District in Congress, in 1837 and 1840. Mr. Gray justly ranks among the ablest jurists in our State, and was appointed Circuit Judge of the Supreme Court of the State of New York in 1846.

In the State Convention of 1801, held to draft a Constitution for the State of New York, Honorable John Patterson was the delegate from Tioga.

At the period of the first settlement of the Chemung Valley, this section was included in Montgomery County (the name of the county having been changed from Tryon in 1784.) In 1784, Tioga was taken from Montgomery, and erected into a separate county. It then included Chemung, which had been formed into townships in the year 1789, and five other towns, and which now embraces Tioga and Broome, and parts of Chemung, and Chenango counties.

In 1792, a part of Chemung was detached established as a separate township under Newtown; and in 1808 the name of the town was changed by act of Legislature, from Newtown to Elmira.

In 1812, when the United States had declared war against Great Britain, to sustain our maritime rights, this region most nobly and patriotically responded to the call that our government then made for troops. Among the men who were most earnest, active, and influential in raising a force to join the American army on the frontiers, Mathew Carpenter, should particularly be named. He was first appointed Brigadier-General, and afterwards advanced to rank of Major-General. General Carpenter had been a soldier in the American army during the Revolution. He had always been one of the most prominent among the public men of this section in contributing his talents and energy to building up and sustaining the pioneer settlements of the Chemung Valley.

In the Convention of 1821, held in Albany, to amend the Constitution of the State of New York, General Carpenter was elected to represent the County of Tioga. He died here, in 1831, at the age of eighty-one years.

In a company raised in the section about Newtown, in the war of 1812, J. Jenkins, of Southport, was appointed Captain; J. Sayers First Lieutenant, and Phineas Catlin, of Catharine, Second Lieutenant.

The earliest newspaper published in Chemung County (then embraced in Tioga) was issued at Newtown; and it was styled *The Telegraph*. In 1816, it was changed to *Vidette*. In 1821, *The Investigator* was commenced at Elmira, and in the same year the name of this newspaper was changed to *The Tioga Register*. Two daily newspapers the *The Advertiser* and the *Gazette*, - both of which are ably sustained in the editorial department, and give an interesting record of current events, - are now published at Elmira.

In 1836, Chemung County was established - the towns within the new county being detached from Tioga County. On the organization of

Chemung County, in 1836, Governor Troop appointed Joseph S. Darling as first judge of the county, and he exercised the judicial duties pertaining to this office until 1849, when he resigned the position. Mr. Darling was succeeded, in 1844, by James Dunn, as first Judge of the County, and held the office until 1846, and here, Mr. Darling again received the appointment as Judge, and performed the labors connected with the office until the new State Constitution went into effect in 1847.

Mr. Darling had settled near Odessa, New York (now in Schuyler County) in 1819, where he still resides. He has now reached the age of eighty-two years. Mr. Darling has been succeeded in this office - first judge of Chemung County - by several men of legal ability, but by none more able than Horace B. Smith.

The Legislature of the State of New York had passed an Act on April 15, 1819, authorizing the construction of the Chemung Canal, to extend from the Chemung River, at Elmira, to Havana; The surveys and estimates for this canal were submitted by Holmes Hutchinson, November 12, 1829. The Chemung Canal, was put under contract in April 1830, at an estimated cost of $291,831.00. The Chemung Canal, with the Feeder Canal that connected it with the Canisteo river near Painted Post (now Corning), and intersected with the canal at Horseheads, was completed on September 10, 1831. The Canal and Feeder Canals required the building of fifty-two locks, seventy-six bridges, etc., and the entire cost of construction was $314,385.51.

The village of Elmira was incorporated in 1815. The Elmira Seminary for Young Ladies commenced about 1819, and I believe is now in prosperous condition. The Elmira Academy, a private institution, has been in successful operation - for many years; and the Elmira Female College, incorporated in 1855, now ranks among the first collegiate institutions of our state.

I cannot attempt the relation of many events of unimportant moment, which have occurred during recent years at Elmira, or in the surrounding region, but I will proceed at once to give some view of the more stirring period in our history connected with the Civil War which was commenced in 1861; though I may only be able to give a brief statement about the actions of prominent men of this section in their noble efforts to sustain the cause of the Union in the midst of the terrible ordeal of civil war.

The Rebellion resulted, unquestionably, from the disappointed ambition of a few political leaders in the Southern States who during many years had been ceaselessly plotting the disruption of the Union as established by the Constitution framed by the men of the Revolution; and then, from the ruins of this noble fabric, these criminal leaders fancied that they should succeed in forming a separate confederacy, in which their own will and caprice would be the supreme law. It was, but the repetition of great crimes hitherto enacted in human history; but I am fully conscious of my inability to portray the magnitude of the crime and madness exhibited by the leaders of the Rebellion of 1801, and I may well adopt the invocation of the great Epic poet as expressed in the numbers of the Iliad:

"Achilles' wrath, the direful spring
Of Grecian woes, O Goddess sing!"

Nevertheless, if the writer of this sketch arrived at an erroneous opinion as to the position occupied by the leading statesmen of our country, and especially as to the part which they respectively had assumed in the opening act of the great drama of civil war, this error did not arise from failure of opportunity to become conversant, either through the medium of personal conversation or by correspondence, with the views entertained respecting the questions involved in this conflict by the principal members of the Executive, Judicial and Legislative Departments of the National Government during the years 1800-1801, including in this number the Lieutenant-General, and other veteran officers of the U. S. Army, eminent Senators, &c.

The unhallowed purposes of treason, the criminal objects of the rebellion, had been openly avowed by political leaders in the spring of 1860. Sagacious and patriotic stales- men of our country fully comprehended the magnitude of the danger which threatened our Republic, although in the new and untried exigencies of public affairs, these patriotic men differed in opinion regarding the better policy, or requisite measures to be adopted. In the Executive Department of the Government, the eminent and illustrious statesman then occupying the position of Chief Magistrate, Mr. Buchanan, had adopted a conciliatory policy, designed to allay political excitement, yet firmly maintaining the authority of the General Government, preparing if it should be assailed, as was afterward done in the attack made by the conspirators upon Fort Sumter, to sustain the supremacy of the Union by all the energy and military power of the government.

A majority of the cabinet were Southern men, but whenever any of these evinced by his active opposition to the patriotic purposes and exertions of the loyal men living in the South, and had shown active sympathy with the conspirators, they were promptly compelled to leave the Cabinet, and their places were at once filled by true men, as; thus, Holt was appointed Secretary of War, and Dix as Secretary of the Treasury, etc. And the result of this policy, in throwing thy responsibility of commencing the war, as assumed by the attack made upon Sumter, giving the weight of moral victory upon the side of the Union, and which exerted an important influence in deciding the course taken by the border States, at once evinced the unswerving integrity, and the comprehensive statesmanship of President Buchanan in this momentous period of our history.

The patriotic men, the true statesmen of our country, at this perilous period, united their earnest efforts - in behalf of the Union, and counseled and labored to secure some adjustment of difficulties, as: had been done at various times in the previous history of our nation, whereby hostile collisions of sections of our country would be avoided- or rather, these noble and patriotic statesmen sought to lay a broad foundation; upon which all truly loyal and conservative men could unite while engaged in the struggle in defense of the Union, and thus the war, which the conspirators had determined to force upon the National Government would be of short duration - terminating with speedy discomfiture and overthrow of the traitors.

For the sacred purpose of devising measures for the support of the Union, a Convention composed of delegates from twenty-one states, met on February 4, 1861, at Washington. This conference included among its members the ablest men of our nation, as Honorable S. P. Chase, from Ohio; General John E. Wool, from New York; and the Honorable Reverdy Johnson, from Maryland. This convention, after ample debate, assumed a conciliatory policy. The Honorable Reverdy Johnson who in 1861 alike as at present, held the distinguished rank as one of the ablest statesmen and jurists of our land, exercised, by the resistless force of his eloquence, unsurpassed in rhetorical beauty, and unequaled in strength of argument, a controlling influence over the deliberations of this important convention. Mr. Johnson now holds the first rank, the preeminent position, as the ablest statesman in the American Senate, where within this proud forum of debate and legislation the illustrious Senator of Maryland has indeed rivaled by his eloquence the lofty reputation acquired here by Webster and by Clay - and, in our own time, by the unequaled statesmanship, eloquence, and wisdom which he has thus brought to the councils of the Republic, has won resplendent fame, whose luster will grow dim only when the firmament itself shall fade away!

The action of the Convention of 1861 could not prevent the rebellion which had been already fully matured by the conspirators; but if all the patriotic, or professed Union men of the nation, had given approval of its platform, the rebellion would have been shorn of its proportions and disarmed of its power.

Among the great men of the Republic, whose long period of eminent public services had rendered their names illustrious in its annals, and who united their earnest efforts in defense of the Union, I have only space to name Honorable Lewis Cass, Honorable J. J. Crittenden, Honorable J. A. Bayard; Messrs. Wayne and Nelson, of the Supreme Court; Generals Scott and Wool; and the Honorable George M. Dallas who had formerly occupied with preeminent ability and honor the important position of Vice-President of the Republic, and as the presiding officer of the Senate in its palmiest days, winning the trophies of unequaled and enduring fame.

The National Administration, in its efforts to sustain the Union intact, had to contend not only with the ceaseless activity of the treasonable conspirators at the South, but also against the evil influence of that class of persons within the North, who were, in reality, looking for the disruption of the Union, as a change bringing to them the

> "Tide in the affairs of men,
> Which, taken at the flood, leads on to fortune."

Thus, a distinguished senator who afterward became a member of Mr. Lincoln's cabinet, treated the idea that any formidable attempt upon the part of the Southerners to dissolve the Union was only fancy, and that "a dozen John Browns could scare them back"; whilst a prominent editor, who has since shown his particular friendship for Davis, and his fellow conspirators in crime, avowed his opposition to any "coercive measures" to sustain the Union.

The administration of President Buchanan, the War Department being under the efficient direction of Holt, had continued steadily to strengthen our national defenses at the most important points, and the Government of the nation, in its unbroken supremacy, was handed over, March 4, 1861, to the succeeding executive administration.

The action subsequently taken by the National administration, upon the event of the attack which was made upon our national forts at Charleston, was precisely like that which would have been pursued, in a similar event, by the administration of President Buchanan. Neither the administration of Mr. Buchanan, nor of Mr. Lincoln, proceeded to inaugurate forcible measures until the leaders of the rebellion had committed an overt act of resistance to the authority and supremacy of the Federal Government.

It will be observed that both of these administrations adopted and pursued practically, the same course. I only give a statement of the facts in the premises.

It may not be improper to mention, that in the most despondent and gloomy period to our nation in the prosecution of the war to suppress the rebellion, when many friends of the Union were almost ready to abandon further conflict as hopeless of success, ex-President Buchanan had thus expressed, to the writer of this sketch, his views of the war:

"The South, unnecessarily and without any adequate provocation, had commenced a war when it may terminate. Heaven only knows, but I hope and trust only upon the restoration of the Union."

These few expressive words covered the whole ground of the great conflict. The earnest devotion that this eminent statesman had evinced for the Union during his long and distinguished career in the public councils of the Republic, as well as throughout the important period of his administration of the National Government, continued unshaken in the darkest hours of the late momentous Civil War. Future history holds the glorious reward of his patriotism and statesmanship.

However, in early 1861, the madness and criminal ambition of Southern leaders precipitating the country into a war; and to the appeal of our government to sustain the Union intact, the people everywhere in the loyal States responded with an enthusiasm only equaled by that which had been displayed by the patriots of the Revolution; and the veteran not less than the eminent Generals, of the war of 1812, and who had also won the laurels of resplendent fame upon the victorious battlefields of Mexico - Scott and Wool- gave their fullest energies to sustain the military supremacy of the Union. And these veteran officers, whose names had been rendered illustrious in the military service of the republic, were most nobly seconded by the heroism and strategic skill displayed by McClellan, by Sherman, and by Grant, until the final triumph of our arms was achieved through the unparalleled energy and military skill, the masterly strategy and brilliant movements of the great captain of the age - General Ulysses S. Grant - whose illustrious achievements have nobly earned the enduring gratitude of his country, not less than the laurels of immortal fame.

The patriotism and noble endurance shown by the American people throughout the progress of the war, became entitled to unmeasured praise, as it indeed constitutes a solid and lasting tribute to the intelligence and virtue of the masses, not less than to the worth and permanence of Republican institutions of government.

Unfortunately the general direction of military affairs, the charge of the War Department connected with the National Government during the civil war - as had previously been the case in the war with Great Britain in 1812- was placed under the control of those who possessed no practical knowledge of the exigencies and requirements of military service. Had the War Department, upon the first outbreak of the rebellion, been at once placed and continued entirely under direction of such an able and skillful military chieftain as Major-General John E. Wool, and our heroic generals and armies in the field been properly supported in the strategic movements which were bravely prosecuted for the suppression of the rebellion, and the military power by which it was sustained, there cannot be the slightest doubt but that the arms and flag of the Republic would have been fully and gloriously triumphant in 1862 - and treason and traitors alike been awarded the due penalty for the blackest crime which earth ever witnessed, and the question settled whether treason is crime- for if there were no living witnesses as to the guilt of the traitors, then would they spring by unnumbered thousands from every battle-field of this civil war, to confront Davis and his fellow conspirators with evidence of their "damning deeds" - and the terrible demon of Disunion be banished from our land forever!

Nor was this section of the State, the region about Elmira, behind any locality of our country in the promptitude and ardor with which it raised volunteers for the army. Among the patriotic men of this section, and I may add of the State, none displayed greater energy in the noble efforts that were made to subserve the cause of the Union, than the Honorable A. S. Diven, of Elmira. Mr. Diven was born in Reading, Pennslyvania, about the year 1810. He read law with Judge Gray, of Elmira, and was a representative in Congress in 1859-1861, where he had shown distinguished legislative ability.

The 107th Regiment of New York Volunteers, of which Robert B. Van Valkenburgh had command as Colonel, and A. S. Diven was the Lieutenant-Colonel, went into service on August 12, 1862, and was engaged in the battle of Antietam on October 12. Diven received the appointment of Colonel of the Regiment, succeeding Colonel Van Valkenburgh in command. In the Battle of Chancellorsville, Colonel Diven, then commanding this Regiment, led his men amid the fiercest conflict, in which he displayed distinguished gallantry, and exercised great judgment in directing his troops. An officer of the Regiment remarked to me, in reference to Colonel Diven's participation in this battle, etc., as follows: "A braver man never lived." In May 1863, Diven received the appointment of Adjutant-General, with the rank of Major, and was placed in charge of the rendezvous for troops at Elmira. He was appointed Brevet Brigadier General on August 30, 1864.

General Diven also had, resulting from his military or official position, a general supervision of the several Enrollment Districts of Western New York, and his administration was marked by great ability and integrity; and in the discharge of his official duties, which were general in their nature and limited in their sphere of action, his course was always marked by the most earnest effort to promote the interests of our country, and to secure impartial justice. In these arduous exertions toward maintaining intact the principles of justice and right in the labors which devolved on General Diven, who in accordance with the provisions of the Enrollment Act could exercise only general jurisdiction, whilst the utmost latitude of authority was vested in the several Provost-Marshals, it is known that General Diven was almost universally and remarkably successful. In no instance, it is believed, where he possessed the power to apply correction, was there any matter brought, to his attention, but that justice was promptly enforced.

Fortunately, the various Enrolling Boards within our State were generally composed of intelligent men, whose official action was free from the taint of corruption; it would not be a matter of surprise, however, that, exceptions existed when the miscreants succeeded in cloaking their villainy from observation and correction. The course pursued by some of the members of the Enrolling Board of the 31st District of New York, has not received its due need of praise. The wonderful achievements of these official personages,

"*Dressed in a little brief authority,*"

had indeed surpassed the brilliant campaigns of Don Quixote and his faithful squire, Sancho Panza --had outdone the renowned exploits of Jack Falstaff - and eclipsed the shrewdness and cunning of Iago. The language which hitherto had been adapted to designate disgusting imbecility, and loathsome vice, and degraded infamy, was yet too poor to reach the lowest depths, until the names of a portion of the Officers of this Board had furnished the requisite synonyms of meanness and squalidity. We can class such foul, disgusting deformities only with the idiot, or with the villain, and it were doubtful which would hold the strongest claim; while to rank such despicable creatures upon an equality with the brute - the beast wallowing in its filth, and the reptile crawling in its slime, alike, would spurn the insult and degradation in being classed upon a level with such vile and loathsome vermin.

The exception above adduced becomes more deeply marked in its infamy because it stands alone; a plague-spot showing more strongly by contrast its own foul, cancerous deformity. It formed an anomaly, for which none but the petty officers of this Enrolling Board - whose individual names I will not drag out of the filth to pollute these pages - were in any sense responsible. The records of human baseness are already sufficiently full without the addition of more foul and blacker names - and which would outrival the lists of the lower regions.

The Honorable A. S. Diven resigned the rank which he had so ably held as Brevet-Brigadier General, in the spring of 1865, and resumed the more retired, but equally honorable professional employments of civil life. In every capacity in which he has been engaged, as a Lawyer, as a Representative in Congress, and as a general in our armies, as well as in the important position which he now occupies as one of the principal officers of the New York & Erie Railroad Company, Mr. Diven has always brought to the discharge of his arduous labors unswerving rectitude and pre-eminent ability, and he has justly acquired a solid and enduring reputation.

The history of the region lying northward of Elmira and toward the Seneca Lake - the valleys through which General Sullivan's army had passed in pursuing the broken and flying bands of Indians in 1779 - and beautiful in its varied and romantic scenery, and rich in its historical lore, including the fascinating legends relating to Catharine Montour, whose true character and life has hitherto been entirely misapprehended. I must reserve for the second part of this sketch, whose continuation will be resumed when a better state of health shall permit, and which will appear in a subsequent volume.

And to this region. bordering upon the majestic Chemung, whose cities and villages have sprung up within the last hundred years from the Wilderness as if by the wand of some God of olden myth, and whose history comes like some fairy tale of the Arabian Nights. I must here bid adieu!

NOTE

The Author of the *Historical Sketch of the Chemung*, has not aimed to write a formal narrative of events which have transpired in the region embraced in his researches, or, in other words, to prepare a "'History" in its usual staid manner or style - but he has designed rather to give a view, a Sketch, of the Past and Present of this interesting region of our country, and in the somewhat desultory style which the poor condition of health would warrant him only in attempting to write. A year has now elapsed since the sketch was prepared, and its statements subjected to the free criticism of the public, and whilst many who were conversant with events narrated have since corroborated its most important statements, but a simple error in the entire narrative has been brought to the Author's attention - although one or two hear-say stories, which the writer had previously found to be unreliable, have been reiterated in other quarters. This one error - or probable error - is the story in regard to Louis Bonaparte having stopped at Elmira, and made a tour in this vicinity, during the period of the visit of the present distinguished Emperor, in America, in 1837. This statement was made in accordance with information which the Author deemed reliable. Nevertheless, the Author feared that there had been some mistake as to identity of the individual who had stopped at Elmira, and the Reverend J. S. C. Abbott, who is fully conversant with the career of Napoleon III, in a letter to the Author of this sketch expresses his belief that Louis Napoleon did not, visit Elmira whilst in the United States in 1837- and the statement of the Reverend Mr. Abbott is also substantially given by Honorable J. T. Headley, in a communication to the Author of this sketch. .

The Author has been able to examine only a portion of the proof-sheets of this sketch, and for any errors which occur, he must ask the indulgence of the reader.

For valuable aid and information which very courteously has been given to the Author whilst pursuing his investigation connected with preparation of both the First and Second Parts of this Sketch, he will beg to express his great obligations to Honorable G. H. McMaster, of Bath: Mrs. Maxwell, (for loan of Historical M.SS of late Honorable Thomas Maxwell) of Elmira; Honorable A. S. Diven, Honorable Charles P. Avery, Honorable William W. Campbell, William C. Bryant, Esq., Captain D. P. Dey, (the gentleman Commander of the Steamer "D. S. Magee") and Reverend Dr. Wilson, President of Geneva College, besides many others; and, to all who have thus given generous aid in facilitating the author's inquiries and work, he returns his sincere thanks.

If this Sketch has incidentally shown that human life, when governed by conscious purpose and effort, controlled by absolute honesty and truth, by refined and pure sensibility of thought and emotion, secures the only noble award truly worthy of the aim and endeavor of man, then the Author is content, and perchance

"Not in vain
He wore his sandal shoon, and scallop shell."

Sunnywild, July 1, 1868

INDEX

Abbott, Rev. J.S.C., 179-180
Abbott, William, 118, 121, 124
Aboriginal, Aborigines, 7, 9, 11, 54, 104, 141
Acwinoshioni [Iroquois] - see also Aquinoshioni, 43, 45
Adams, President John, 104, 158
Afton, New York, 63
Albany, New York, 11, 29, 33, 75, 85, 87, 95, 107, 109, 121-122, 124, 126, 133, 137, 166
Alden, Colonel, 90-91
Algonquin, 11, 45
Allansan, Lieutenant, 48
Allegany, Allegheny, Alleghenies, 10, 27, 30, 39, 104
American Revolution - see also Revolutionary, 7-9, 17, 24, 29, 38-40, 46-47, 49, 68, 70-72, 81, 85, 87, 95-97, 99-100, 103-104, 107, 109, 141, 156, 158-160, 166, 168, 173
Americans, 45, 76-77, 81, 93, 101, 107
Andes, New York, 69
Antietam, Battle of, 175
Apple Hill, 125, 129, 133
Aquinoshioni - see also Acwinoshioni, 14
Argyle, Duke of, 134-135
Argyleshire, 135
Arnold, Benedict, 29
Aspenwall, Dr., 163

Atatasho, 156
Athens, Pennsylvania, 50, 164
Aupaumet, Hendrick, 149
Avery, Charles P., 50

Bainbridge, New York, 63
Baker, Caleb, 160
Baker, Judge Samuel, 23, 29
Baldwin, Caleb, 160-161
Baldwin, Colonel Thomas, 49, 52, 156-157
Baldwin, Henry, 160
Baldwin, Isaac, 160
Baldwin, J., 163
Baltimore, Maryland, 24, 27
Bancroft, George, 140, 147
Bancroft, R. , 163
Baptist, 26, 57, 63, 123, 160, 162
Barker, Judge, 23
Barnes, Timothy, 121
Barstow, G.W., 161, 165
Bates, Usual, 158
Bath Gazette, The, 30
Beal family, 85
Bennet, S., 25-26
Bennett, E., 160
Bennett, Ephriam, 49
Bennett, Green, 49-50
Benton, Thomas H., 57
Berwick, Maine, 37
Big Flats, New York, 158
Binghamton, New York, 55-57
Blacksnake, Governor, 103-104
Blake, D.T., 29
Blurker, Captain J., 75
Bolles, L.M., 123

Bonaparte, Louis Napoleon, 162, 179-180
Boone, Captain Hawkins, 21, 23
Boone, Daniel, 23
Boston, Massachusetts, 49
Bower, James, 160
Bowers, John M., 125
Braddock, 39, 75
Bradford, Massachusetts, 49
Brainard Hotel, Elmira, 150
Brandywine, Pennsylvania, 38
Brant, Joseph [Thayandanegea], 34, 41, 44-45, 47, 50, 54-55, 68, 73, 75-82, 88-90, 100-103, 106-107
Brett, J.H., 69
Brick, Elijah, 160
Brickville, New York, 160
Brooks, T., 163
Broome County, New York, 20, 56-57, 62, 71, 165
Brown, Charles Brockden, 139
Bryant, William Cullen, 6, 139, 143, 147, 180
Buchanan, James, 58, 169-170, 172
Buffalo, New York, 50, 161
Burgoyne, General, 78, 81, 108
Burlington, New Jersey, 113, 137
Butler, Colonel John, 22, 34, 41, 51, 77, 80, 90, 100, 107
Butternuts, New York, 124, 127

Calkins, Frederick, 23
Cameron, Charles, 28
Cameron, Mrs. Charles, 94, 97
Campbell, Colonel Samuel, 92
Campbell, James S., 34
Campbell, Robert, 28, 94-95, 97-100, 104, 125, 133-135, 140
Campbell, William W., 87-88, 110, 180
Canada, 16-17, 28, 34, 39, 97, 108
Canadesaga, 153

Canajoharie, New York, 40, 100, 114, 117
Canandaiagua, New York, 17
Canisteer, 26
Canisteo, New York, 8, 17, 19, 21-22, 24-27, 167
Cantine, John, 158
Carey, Alice, 139
Carey, Phebia, 139
Carpenter, Mathew, 166
Carr, Mr., 85
Cartier, Jacques, 14-15, 41
Cass, Lewis, 14, 58, 171
Catharine's Town, 47-49, 52, 149
Catharine, New York (present town), 166
Catherine Creek, 17, 53
Catlin, Phineas, 166
Catskill Mountains, 70, 86
Cayuga, Cayugas, 17, 19, 47, 52, 85, 149, 153-154
Chamberlain, J., 163
Champlain, Samuel de, 15, 46
Chancellorsville, Battle of, 175
Charleston, South Carolina, 172
Charlevoix, 15
Chastelleaux, 116
Chautauqua, New York, 74
Chemung, New York, 3-4, 7-8, 10, 12, 14, 16, 18-20, 22-28, 30-32, 34, 36-38, 40-44, 46-56, 58, 60, 62, 64, 66, 68, 70-72, 74, 76, 78, 80, 82, 84, 86, 88, 90, 92, 94, 96, 98, 100-102, 104, 106, 108, 110, 112, 114, 116, 118, 120, 122, 124, 126, 128, 130, 132, 134, 136, 138, 140, 142, 144, 146, 148, 150, 152-154, 156-160, 162-168, 170, 172, 174, 176-180, 182, 184, 186, 188, 190, 192, 194, 196, 198, 200, 202, 204
Chenango, New York, 56-57, 63, 66-67, 71, 158, 165
Cherry Valley, New York, 31, 34-35, 38, 68, 73, 75, 86-96, 98-99, 103, 113, 115, 121, 132, 134-135, 163
Chevalier, 117
chiefs, chieftains, 20-22, 41, 45, 81, 85, 90, 135, 150, 153, 174

children, 33-34, 50, 77, 91-94, 97, 101-102, 155
Church, churches, 63, 87, 121-123, 127, 160, 162-163
Churchill, Lemuel, 159
Claremont, New Hampshire, 133
Clarke, Reverend Thomas, 163
Clinton, DeWitt, 67
Clinton, General James, 39-40, 42, 44, 63, 67, 70, 92, 95, 97, 107-108, 110-111, 113-116, 156, 158
Clinton, Governor George, 35, 40, 63, 95, 107, 156, 158
Clinton, Sir Henry, 70, 108
Clyde, Colonel, 92-93
Cobleskill, New York, 100
Colden, Cadwalder, 111
Colonial, 15, 17, 19-21, 46-47, 70, 75, 107, 112
Colonies, colony, 15, 63, 70, 107, 112
Columbia County, New York, 132, 143
Columbiad, 32
Columbus, Christopher, 13
Concord, Massachusetts, 49
Conewango, 73
Confederacy, confederate, 8-9, 14, 16, 35, 38, 43, 45, 54, 70, 101, 156, 168, 187
Congregational, 29
Conhocton (Cohocton) River, New York, 8, 19, 21-22, 24-25, 27-28
Connecticut, 33, 56, 63, 119-120
Continental Congress, 37-39, 54, 61-62, 84, 107-109, 114, 125-126, 128, 133, 160, 164-165, 175, 177
Cooper's Patent, 112-113
Cooper, Anna, 127
Cooper, George D., 29, 112-113
Cooper, Isaac, 126
Cooper, J. Fennimore, 55, 120, 125, 129, 137-147
Cooper, Richard Fenniore, 125
Cooper, William, 116, 119-120
Cooperstown Classical and Military Academy, 123
Cooperstown Federalist, The, 124

Cooperstown, New York, 55, 111-114, 116, 118-129, 132-137, 143-144
Corlaer, Governor, 85
Corn Planter (Gai-ant-wake), 41, 102, 150-151, 154
Corning Democrat, The, 25
Corning Journal, The, 25
Corning, New York, 22, 24-25, 167
Cortland, New York, 129
Cory, Oliver, 120-121
Cory, Oliver, 120
Coryell, Emanuel, 161, 164
Council, councils, 14, 19-20, 33, 57-58, 61-62, 77, 86, 94, 110, 149-151, 153-154, 156, 171, 173
Country Magazine, The, 124
Covell, Lyman, 159, 163
Cowanesque, Pennsylvania, 23
Cox, Colonel, 76
Craig, Andrew, 113
Cricket, The, 116
Crippen, Schuyler, 134
Crittenden, J.J., 171
Crogan, Colonel, 75, 112-113
Crooker, George A.S., 63, 65, 72
Crooker, George A.S., 72
Crosby, Enoch, 141
Crosby, K., 25-26, 141
Cruger, Daniel, 28-29
Cully, Mr., 85

Dallas, George M., 57, 171
Darling, Joseph S., 167
Davis, Jefferson, 172, 174
de Chastelleaux, Marquis, 116
De la Barne, 46
De Nonville, Marquis, 16, 46
De Soto, Hernando, 74

Declaration of Independence, 70
Deer Slayer, 140, 143
Delancy, Susan, 138
Delaware, Delawares, 19-20, 55, 67-69, 82, 85, 100, 152
Delhi, New York, 69
Denmark, 28
Dewey, Joshua, 120
DeWittsburg (Elmira). New York, 157
Dey, D.P., 180
Dickinson, D.S., 55, 57-62, 161, 165
Diven, 161
Diven, A.S., 163, 175-177, 180
Dix, John A., 133
Dix, Secretary, 169
Drake, John R., 161
Draper, Amos, 56
Duke of Orleans - Louis Philippe, 161
Dunlap, Reverend Samuel, 87, 91
Dunn, James, 167
Dunn, William, 28, 160-161
Dutchess County, New York, 141

Eagle Hotel, Otsego, New York, 128
Earl of Bath, 27
Eaton, B., 24
Eaton, H.P., 113
Eddie, James, 30
Edgewater, Cooperstown, New York, 118, 126
Edsell, Richard, 158
Edwards, Edward, 165
Edwards, George C., 163
Edwards, Preston, 55, 163, 165
Ellicottville, New York, 28
Ellison, Reverend, 137
Ellison, Thomas, 122-123

Ellison, William, 118-119
Elmira Academy, 167
Elmira Advertiser, The, 166
Elmira Female College, 167
Elmira Gazette, The, 166
Elmira Investigator, The , 166
Elmira Seminary for Young Ladies, 167
Elmira Telegraph, The , 166
Elmira Vidette, The , 166
Elmira, Conongue Street in , 150
Elmira, New York - see also Newtown, 31, 47, 49-50, 52, 56, 150, 152, 157-158, 160-161, 163-168, 174-175, 177, 179-180, 187
Emperor, 162, 179
Empire, 9, 14, 16, 41
England, 10, 27, 57-58, 70, 109, 137-138, 147, 157
Enos, J., 66
Episcopal, 122, 127, 163
Ernst, John Frederick, 122
Erwin, A., 24
Erwin, J., 163
Erwin, L., 24
Europe, 10-11, 13, 95, 109, 137-138, 143-144
Everett, Doctor, 50
Everett, Edward, 12, 29, 107, 165
expedition, expeditions, 7, 12, 15-16, 19-20, 29, 31-32, 34-35, 37-43, 46-48, 50, 52-55, 70-71, 74-75, 90, 100-101, 103, 107-108, 110, 114, 152-153
exploration, 25, 153

Farmer, Brother (Ho-nai-ye-wus), 149
Feeder Canal, Elmira NY, 167
Fish Carrier (O-jea-geh-ta), 149
Fish, Nicolas, 158
Fitch, John, 164
Floridas, 12, 74

flotilla, 111, 115
Fonda, J.G., 120
Foote, Isaac, 66
Foote, Isaac, 66
Fort du Quense, 17
Fort Edward, 107
Fort Grounds, 68
Fort Johnson, 20-21
Fort Plain, 54, 102, 127
Fort Schuyler (or Fort Stanwix), 21, 35, 62-63, 75, 78, 80-82, 85, 114, 117, 149-150
Fort Sumter, 169
Fort William and Mary, 37-39
fort, forts, 33, 88-91, 93, 99, 172
fortification(s), 17, 30, 43, 49, 51, 66, 84, 88, 152
France, 15-16, 19, 125, 144
Francis, J.W., 146
Franklin, Governor William (NJ), 112
Frazier, General, 141
Freeling's Fort, 21, 23
Freeman's Journal, 124, 133
Frontenac, Count, 16, 39, 46
frontier, 17, 23, 54-55, 85, 88, 96, 100, 103, 107, 166

Gai-ant-wake - see Corn Planter, 151
Ganienkeh - tribe, 94
Gansevoort, Colonel, 78, 86
Gates, General, 37, 109
Genesee Advertiser, 30
Genesee, New York, 24, 27, 30, 37, 48, 53
Geneva, New York, 30, 53, 94, 161, 180
Gerey, Elbridge, 54
German Flatts, New York, 20, 35, 38, 103
Germantown, Pennsylvania, 38
Gertrude of Wyoming, 31, 104

Gillett, Reverend P.G., 163
Glen Mary on Owego Creek, 56
Goethe, 139, 145
Goff, Reverend Roswell, 160, 162
Goldsborough, Thomas, 163
Gordon, 103
Gorham, Nathaniel, 24, 26-27, 149
Goshen, New York, 101
Government, 59, 97, 103, 108, 112, 125, 131, 149, 151, 154, 166, 169-170, 172-174
Governor, 16, 20, 28, 40, 63, 81, 85-87, 95, 97, 103-104, 112, 123, 127-128, 156, 158, 167
Gravers, Reverend F.W., 163
Gray, Hiram, 165
Green, Josiah, 158
Greene, New York, 50, 63, 65, 67, 139
Griffin, Benjamin, 124
Griffin, Joseph, 121
Grosvenor, Captain, 125
Guild, Israel, 118-119

Haight, S.H., 161, 163
Haight, S.T., 29
Hall, The, 119, 144
Halleck, Fitz Greene, 32, 139, 143
Hamilton, New York, 66
Hanondaganius, 150
Hardenburg Patent, 68
Hare, Lieutenant, 115
Harper, Alexander, 68
Harper, Colonel John, 68
Harpersfield, New York, 68
Harris, William, 23
Hartwick, John C., 112-113
Harvey, Benjamin, 164

Hathorn, John, 158
Haudenosaunee, 155
Havana [Montour Falls], New York, 47, 149, 154, 161, 167
Hawley, Gideon, 55, 111
Headley, J.T., 180
Heckwelder, 33
Heller, E., 163
Hendy, Colonel John, 156-157, 159-160
Hennepin, Father, 15
Hepburn, S., 157
Herkimer County, New York, 66
Herkimer, General, 35, 68, 74, 76-84, 107
Herring, Francis, 124
Hiakatoo, 21
Hiawatha, 14, 156
Hill, C., 63
Hiller, Joseph, 160
Hillsdale, New York, 132
Hincherman, Joseph, 158
Hinchman, Dr. Joseph, 157, 163-164
Ho-nai-ye-wus (see also Farmer's Brother), 149
Hochelega, 11
Hog Back Hill, 48-50, 152
Hollenback, Colonel Matthias, 150, 158, 163
Hollenback, J., 163
Holt, Secretary of War, 169, 172
Honeoye, New York, 53
Hornell, Judge George, 26
Horseheads, New York, 53, 167
Horton. W., 69
Housatonic, 149
Howard, John, 121, 124
Howard, Nathan, 121
Howe, Lord, 107
Howe, Reverend, 57
Howell, Edward, 29

Howell, N.W., 29
Howell, Nathaniel, 160
Hubley, Colonel, 42
Hudson Valley, 70-71, 86, 104, 107
Hulburt, C., 24
Hunter Race, 14, 45
Huntington, Captain S., 124
Hutchinson, Holmes, 167

Impartial Observer, The, 124
Indian, Indians, 9-12, 14, 16-17, 19-25, 27, 31-35, 37-45, 47-50, 52-55, 63, 66-69, 71-81, 84-85, 89-96, 100-103, 105, 107, 110-112, 140, 149-153, 155-156, 177
Indiana, 75
Ireland, 24, 75, 157
Iroquois, 8-12, 14-16, 20, 35, 37, 39, 41, 43-46, 53-54, 76-79, 81, 100-105, 110, 114, 149, 151-156

Jamison, Captain J., 25
Jay, Governor (NY), 156
Jefferson, Thomas, 153
Jenkins, J., 166
Jenkins, William, 150
Jericho, New York, 158
Johnson's Hall, 20, 41, 68, 85
Johnson, Colonel Guy, 19, 41, 75
Johnson, Sir John, 41, 47, 101-102
Johnston, Reverend William, 67, 76
Johnstone, James, 27
Jones, D. , 163
Jones, David, 29-30

Kaensataque, 17
Kanacto, or Knacto, 17, 21

Kanadasaga, 53, 94
Kanantage, 17
Kanesto - see also Canisteo, 17
Kanisteo - see also Canisteo, 19-20
Kaygen, 17
Kellogg, Reverend Nathan, 63
Kendais, 17
Kennedy, John P., 140
Kent, Chancellor, 143
Kent, Moss, 120
Kersey, William, 29-30
Ketchum, S., 63
Keuka Lake (Crooked Lake), 30
Kimms, J.R., 54
King Silberry, 10
King, Rufus, 61
Kingston, New York, 69-70
Kline House, Elmira NY, 159, 161-162
Knox, Judge, 24
Knoxville, 24
Konkle, John, 158

La Fayette, General, 88, 109
La Fayette, Marquis de, 144
Lake Champlain, 11, 117
Lake Erie, 75
Lake Ontario, 17, 117
Lakelands (on Otsego Lake), 118, 125
Lamb, P., 69
Leatherstocking, 141-142
Lebanon, Connecticut, 120
Lee, Elisha, 150
Legislature, 56, 84, 120-121, 126-127, 158, 160, 164, 166-167
Leland, J., 66
Leonard, Joseph, 56

Lewis, Governor, 127
Lexington, Battle of, 151
Lincoln, Abraham, 172
Lindesay, John, 86
Lindley, Colonel, 30
Lindley, Eleazer, 150
Livingston County, New York, 27
Logan, 154
London, 27
Londonderry, New Hampshire, 87, 135
Loomis, B., 63
Loop, Peter, 157, 159, 163
Louis, Philippe (Duke of Orleans), 161-162
Louisburg, Nova Scotia, 41
Lowe, Cornelius, 159
Lumbard, D.C., 25
Lundy's Lane (Niagara Falls, New York), 51
Lutheran, 122

Madison County, New York, 66
Magee, D.S., 180
Manor House (Cooperstown), 119
Marcy, 61
Martin, General, 72
Maryland, 24, 28, 58, 170-171
Massachusetts, 26, 49, 56, 85, 126, 151
Mathews, Vincent, 29, 160, 163-165
Matthews, Selah, 159, 161, 163
Maxwell, Alexander, 157
Maxwell, General, 40, 42, 44, 48-50
Maxwell, Guy, 157-158, 163-165
Maxwell, Thomas, 153, 164, 180
Mayall, Joseph, 96
Mayflower, 74
McBratney, Jane, 157

McClellan, 173
McClure, George, 28-29
McDonald, Reverend John, 122
McDowell, Captain D., 160, 165
McElwn, H., 28
McKean, Captain, 90
McKinsie, D., 28
McMaster, G.H., 180
McMaster, James, 56, 164
McPherson Clan, 157
Mead, Eli, 23
Mercer, General, 156
Metcalf, Elijah, 125-126
Metcalf, Sherman, 28
Metropolitan Hall, 147
Mexico, 173
Miami tribe, 150
Michigan, 49-50
Middlebury, Vermont, 129
Middlefield, New York, 88, 113
Middletown (near Elmira), 47
Milford, New York, 85
Militia, militia, 76, 78, 80, 82, 101, 107-108, 124, 156
Miller, General, 48
Miller, John, 118, 126, 158-159, 161
Miner, 33-34
Minisink, New York, 38, 100, 103
Mississippi, 11, 67
Mitchell, Mrs., 91, 115
Mohawk, Mohawks, 34, 40, 54, 68, 71, 73, 76, 78, 82, 86, 89-90, 94, 96, 99-102, 104, 106, 108, 114-115, 117
Mohican, Mohicans, 140, 142-143, 149
Monmouth, Battle of, 156
Monongahela River, 39
Monroe County, New York, 27
Monster Brant, The, 41, 104

Montcalm, 15
Montgomery County, New York, 56, 68, 87-88, 156, 165
Montgomery, General, 39, 108
Montour Falls - see also Catharine's Town or Havana, 47, 154
Montreal, Quebec, 16-17, 34, 94-95
Moore, Mrs., 94, 139
Morehouse, E.B., 128, 132-134
Morell, George, 135
Morley, Reverend, 121
Morris, Governor, 81
Morris, Jacob, 124, 135
Morris, Robert, 27, 29
Morris, Thomas, 161
Morton, Dr. S.G., 12
mound, mounds, 9-10, 12, 66-67, 152-153
Mount Vernon, Virginia, 161
Mountsponsier, Duke de, 161
Mulford, Mr., 85
Murdoch, Reverend D., 162

Nash, Reverend D., 127
Nelson, Samuel, 128-133, 171
New Hampshire, 37, 54, 87, 133, 135
New Jersey, 24, 28, 112-113, 119-120, 137, 149, 151
New York & Erie Railroad, 177
Newberry (spy), 115
Newbury (Tory), 92
Newport, Expedition against, 38
Newspapers, 24, 30, 124, 166
Newtown (Elmira), 47, 49-52, 56, 149-151, 154, 156-166
Niagara, New York, 15, 17, 29, 34, 41, 51, 53, 68, 94
Nichols, Thomas, 149
Niles, Reverend John, 29
Noah, Donald, 122
Northumberland, 27-28, 157
Norwich, New York, 66-67

O-jea-geh-ta (Fish Carrier), 149
Ocyendahit, 17
Odessa, New York, 167
Ohio, 11, 49, 75, 153, 170
Oneida, Oneidas, 16, 77, 117
Onondaga, Onondagas, 12, 14-16, 19-20, 75, 85, 114
Ontario County, New York, 23, 27, 29-30, 153
Ontario, Canada, 9
Oquago (Windsor, New York), 20, 71, 75
Oriskany, New York, 35, 78, 82
Oswego, New York, 17, 29, 77-78, 102
Otego, New York, 88, 111
Otsego Examiner, 124
Otsego Herald, 124
Otsego Republican, 124
Otsego, New York, 40, 69, 71-75, 82, 86-88, 96, 98, 110-120, 124-128, 133-135, 137, 141, 143-145
Owego, New York, 55-56, 158
Oxford, New York, 66

Paine, Brinton, 160
Painted Post Herald, 25
Paris, France, 15, 143
Parr, Major, 42-43
Parshall, Israel, 158
Partridge, Samuel, 165
patent, 75, 85, 87, 112-113, 121
Pathfinders, 143
Patterson, Benjamin, 23-24
Patterson, John, 57, 161, 164-165
Penn, William, 33, 85
Pennsboro, Pennsylvania, 75
Pennsylvania, Pennsylvanians, 22, 33, 39, 49-50, 56, 58, 75, 103, 154, 157-158, 163-164, 175
Perry, T.M., 163

Phelps, Oliver, 24, 26-27, 149
Philadelphia, Pennyslvania, 27-28, 150, 161-162
Philippe, Louis - Duke of Orleans, 161-162
Phinney, Elihu, 124
Physician, physicians, 120, 146, 163
Pickering, Colonel, 50, 149-151, 154
pioneer, pioneers, 7-8, 23-24, 26, 28, 30, 50, 54, 56, 63, 68, 71-74, 76, 118, 135, 140-143, 150, 156-159, 166
Pomeroy, Mr., 126
Ponchet, Captain, 17
Porter, Judge, 29
Portsmouth, New Hampshire, 37
postmaster, 28, 121, 151
Pouchet, 21
Pratt, Joel, 29
Prattsburg, New York, 29
Precaution, 138-139, 143
Prentice, John H., 132-133
Prentiss, John, 128
Presbyterian, 121-122, 162
presidents, 61, 104-105, 127-129, 132-133, 135, 143, 151, 158, 170-172, 180
Preston, 55
Princeton, New Jersey, 117, 149, 156
prisoner, prisoners, 34, 68, 90-94, 97, 100, 114, 160-161
Proctor, Colonel, 40, 42, 44, 150
Pultney, Pultney Estate, 27, 29
Purdy, J., 163
Putnam, 141

Quebec, 15-17, 27, 29, 41
Queen Catharine Montour, 20, 177
Queen Esther, 33-34

raft, 24, 28
Ramsey, David, 87
Rangers, 90
Rankle, Aaron, 163
Red Jacket [Sa-go-ye-wa-tha], 149
Revolutionary War, 22-23, 34, 49-50, 56, 68, 70-72, 88, 96, 98, 103, 109, 149, 158-159, 161
Reynolds, J., 163
Rhode Island, 38
Robinson, J., 163
Rogers, H.W., 29
Roseboom, T., 86
Ross, James, 163-164
Rumsey, Caroline, 30
Rumsey, Jennie, 30
Russel, John, 125
Russel, Judge, 129

Sa-go-ye-wa-tha (see also Red Jacket), 149
Sachem, sachems, 20, 69, 85, 103-105, 151, 154
Sakima,ing, 74
Salem, Massachusetts, 151
Salem, New York, 72
Sandford, General, 123
Saratoga, New York, 82, 103, 109, 141
savage, savages, 22, 32, 44, 79-80, 90-94, 96, 100, 102-103, 107
Sayers, Captain J., 166
Scarsdale, New York, 138
Schenectady, New York, 91, 117, 125
Schoharie County, New York, 35, 54, 100-103
School, schools, scholars, 9-10, 58, 74, 87, 91, 120-123, 137
Schoolcraft, H.R., 10, 54, 103, 110
Schuyler, General Phillip, 40, 74-75, 78, 107
Scotland, 28, 87, 134-135, 157, 162
Scott, Christian, 159, 163

Sedgwick, (Lawyer), 161
Seneca, Senecas, 8, 13, 16-17, 19-22, 48, 53, 71, 81, 91, 94, 101-104, 110, 149-151, 153-154, 177
settlement, 19, 21, 23, 26, 28, 33-35, 38, 46, 54-57, 63, 68, 71-74, 76, 85, 87-88, 96, 98, 100-103, 107, 112-113, 118, 126, 135-136, 156, 159-160, 165-166
settler, settlers, 24, 26, 54, 63, 68, 72-73, 77, 85, 102, 141, 159-160
Seward, Hector, 150-151
Shamokin, Pennsylvania, 154
Shankland, Robert, 95
Shankland, Thomas, 95-96
Shawnee tribe, 19
Sheather, John, 29
sheriffs, 66, 69, 120, 158-159, 164-165
Sherman, 173
Sidney, New York, 67
Silliman, Benjamin, 9
Simcoe, Governor, 28
Simpson, Bishop, 123
Smead, Benjamin, 30
Smith, Horace B, 167
Snyder, 115
Sodus, New York, 28
Southport (Elmira), New York, 166
Sparks, Jared, 10, 38
Spencer, (Lawyer), 161
Spencer, New York, 56
Sprague, William, 124
Springfield, New York, 88, 90, 114-115
St. Lawrence, 9, 11, 14, 17, 41
St. Leger, or Léger, 34, 78, 108
Starrett, Robert, 159
Stephens, J., 26
Stephens, Uriah, 25
Steuben County, New York, 9, 22-23, 26-27, 29-30, 109
Steuben Courier, The, 30

Stower, John, 159, 162
Street, Alfred B., 16
Strong, Joseph, 120-121
Stuart, William, 29
Sunnywild, 180
Susquehanna, 8, 17, 20-23, 27, 31, 33-34, 39-40, 48, 55-57, 62-63, 67-68, 70-72, 74-76, 82, 85-86, 90, 94-96, 98, 100, 102, 110-112, 115-118, 124-125, 141, 152-155, 162
Switch, The, 124

Tah-hi-ho-gah (Tioga), 50
Talleyrand, 24, 63, 127
Taronyawagan, 14
Tavern, taverns, 23, 26, 28, 118, 120, 159, 162
Teacher, teachers, 120-121, 123
TenBrock, Abraham, 120
Teyewarunte, 19
Thaggen, 17
Thatcher, Daniel, 162
Thayandenagea [Joseph Brant], 41, 68, 77, 102-103, 107
Thurston, A. S., 163
Tienaderha, 74
Tioga, 17, 19, 21, 23, 30, 34, 39-40, 42-43, 47-50, 53, 56, 66, 71, 94, 102, 110, 116, 149-150, 156-159, 161, 164-166
Tioga Register, The, 166
Tocsin, 124
Tories, 21, 32, 54, 68, 77, 79-80, 91-92, 100, 107-108
Tracy, William, 66
Treaty, treaties, 21, 63, 75, 85, 104, 150-151, 154
Tremain, D., 63
Trenton, New Jersey, 156
Tribe, tribes, 7, 10-12, 19-20, 22, 39, 41, 54-55, 77, 94, 102-103, 110, 150-151, 153-155
tribunal, 130-131, 133
Troupe, Robert, 29

Tryon County, New York, 34, 38, 72, 74, 82, 87-88, 98-100, 102, 107-110, 140, 165
Turner, Levi, 133
Tuscarora, Tuscaroras, 14, 153
Tuttle, S., 163

Ulster County, New York, 38-39, 69-70, 82, 100, 103
Unadilla, New York, 24, 38, 71-72, 74-77, 84-85, 88, 90, 103
Urbana, New York, 23

Van Buren, President, 61, 127-129, 132-133
Van Ness, (Jurist), 161
Van Rensselaer, General, 127
Van Schick, Colonel, 114
Van Valkenburgh, Robert, 86, 114, 175
Vandreville, M. de, 16
Vermont, 23, 63, 129
Verplanck, William, 29, 143
Village of the Plains (Bath, NY), 28
Vineland, 12
Virginia, 23, 28, 141, 153-154, 157

Warwick, New York, 49
Washington, George, 28-29, 37-40, 55, 72, 95-98, 104-105, 108, 116-117, 127, 129, 139, 150-151, 161, 170
Watch Tower, The, 124
Wattle's Ferry, New York, 24
Wayne County, New York, 27
Welles, Henry, 29
Welles, John, 91
Welles, Miss Jane, 91
Welles, Robert, 91
Wellsburg, New York, 160

Westchester, New York, 138, 143
Western Advertiser, 124
Wheeler, Silas, 29
White, James, 118
Wielaud, 139
Wilkes-Barre, Pennsylvania, 53, 162-163
Willet, Colonel, 80-81, 114
Williamson, Captain Charles, 27-29
Willis, N.P., 56
Wilson, Reverend Dr., 180
Windsor, New York, 20, 55-56
Winter, J., 24
Wismer, Colonel, 101
Wisner, Jeffrey, 157
Wolfe, General, 15
Wood Creek, New York, 117
Woodhall, Nathaniel, 107
Woodworth, (Jurist), 161
Wool, John, 170-171, 173-174
Wooster, E., 68, 108
Worcester, New York, 133-134
Wormwood, Lieutenant, 89-90
Wyncoop, William, 160
Wyoming, Battle of - Pennsylvania, 22, 31-34, 49, 56-57, 90, 103-104, 106, 110, 149, 158

Yale, 9, 137

Reprinted by
New York History Review Press

Why do we digitally restore and reprint vintage books?

Plain and simple - if we don't, who will? We believe a digitally restored book should have the appearance that it would have had if it never needed mending. It should have as much of the original material as is possible to use and still maintain the usability of the book. All new work should be in keeping with the style and the time in which the book was produced.

Our conservators maintain the integrity of the book while making it usable in the present, and preserving the content for posterity. Digital methods have made the art of book restoration a much simpler task, allowing restoration artists to work on a digital image instead of the original photograph, slide or negative. Our books have been restored to an excellent state without altering the original concept. Old books can be revived by "cleaning up" mildew, water stains, spots, and tears.

Our printing method uses state of the art technology and the Internet provides 24/7 world wide access to find these fine old books.

Thank you for your interest!

NewYorkHistoryReview.com

More from New York History Review

The Elmira Prison Camp
by Clay Holmes & Diane Janowski

*In Their Honor: Soldiers of the Confederacy -
The Elmira Prison Camp*
by Diane Janowski

Harper's New York and Erie Railroad Guide, 1851
by William MacLeod

Zim's Foolish History of Elmira
by Eugene Zimmerman

*To War and Back: The Lightning Division -
Carl Albert Janowski's war diary 1918 - 1919*
by Diane Janowski

Brief History of Chemung County
by Ausburn Towner

www.ingramcontent.com/pod-product-compliance
Lightning Source LLC
Chambersburg PA
CBHW032253150426
43195CB00008BA/433